The
Workplace

Questions
Women Ask

The Workplace Questions Women Ask

Judith Briles

Luci Swindoll

Mary Whelchel

Christianity Today, Inc.

in conjunction with

MULTNOMAH
Portland, Oregon

Cover design by Bruce De Roos
THE WORKPLACE: QUESTIONS WOMEN ASK
© 1992 by Christianity Today, Inc.
Published by Multnomah Press
10209 SE Division Street
Portland, Oregon 97266

Multnomah Press is a ministry of
Multnomah School of the Bible
8435 NE Glisan Street
Portland, Oregon 97220

Printed in the United States of America.

Library of Congress Cataloging-in-Publication Data
Briles, Judith.
  The workplace : questions women ask / Judith Briles, Luci Swindoll, Mary Whelchel.
      p.   cm. — (Friend to friend)
  Includes bibliographical references.
  ISBN 0-88070-502-7
  1. Women, Christian—Conduct of life, 2. Women, Christian-Employment.
3. Witness bearing (Christianity)   I. Swindoll, Luci. 1932- . II. Whelchel, Mary. III. Title. IV. Series.
BJ1610.B75 1992
650.1'3'082—dc20   92-26058
                                                                 CIP

92 93 94 95 96 97 98 99 00 01 - 10 9 8 7 6 5 4 3 2 1

CONTENTS

SECTION THREE
Putting Christian Character to Work

Introduction

THE WORKING WOMAN'S BLUEPRINT

 t's been said the Bible is curiously silent about the workplace. But is it? Consider for a moment a few broad definitions of the workplace. It's relationships. It's people. It's decisions. It's choices. And when we think of it in those terms, we begin to realize the Bible is anything but silent on the workplace.

Our work, whether it takes place in an office setting, the classroom, or the outdoors, includes all the essentials to test, develop, and live out our Christian faith. Granted, it is tough at times to balance our multiple roles or work alongside a co-worker whose values differ radically from our own. But we shouldn't shy away from such challenges—for the rewards of being a working Christian woman are plentiful. As part of the work world—the mission field of the nineties—we should delight in those daily opportunities that sharpen our faith, that make us better messengers for the Lord.

As contributor Mary Whelchel notes, "The workplace is a battlefield where you either die or grow. But for those who latch on to the Lord, it's an environment where you'll be challenged to grow in your faith in exciting ways."

So how can we as Christian women thrive and be strong witnesses in the workplace? How do we make career decisions that are in line with God's will? How do we show Christian compassion and love to a co-worker whose behavior causes us to grit our teeth? How do we share Christ and draw others to him while at the same time performing our daily responsibilities?

In this book, Judith Briles, Luci Swindoll, and Mary Whelchel call upon their years of experience in the business world to offer practical and proven insights on handling the 101 challenges that face Christian working women today. Each contributor generously shares her wisdom and godly counsel—her triumphs as well as her trials.

We hope their heartfelt answers to the seventeen questions that make up this book will better equip you as well as encourage you to be a shining light in the marketplace—a marketplace that, in Luci's words, "Is dying for believers."

The chapters in this book are based on personal interviews conducted in June 1991, as well as follow-up telephone interviews. Also featured in each chapter are excerpts from the pages of *Today's Christian Woman* magazine; as well as a section entitled, "Make It Happen," offering practical ways you can quickly and easily implement the specific suggestions made in each chapter.

About the Contributors

Judith, Luci, and Mary are pioneers of sorts, having held positions or ventured into careers previously not occupied by women. Their advice comes not from lofty philosophies or ideals but from the day-in and day-out struggles of balancing work, personal life, and faith.

Judith Briles lives in Denver, Colorado, and maintains a packed speaking schedule that takes her across the United States and Europe. When not traveling, Judith devotes her time to writing books. To date, she has ten titles to her credit, including

When God Says No (Word) and *Woman to Woman: From Sabotage to Support* (New Horizon Press). In addition, she is host of an afternoon radio show in the Denver area and appears regularly on national TV.

Judith began her career as a stockbroker with E. F. Hutton and from there pursued a career as a financial consultant with her business, The Briles Group, Inc. She's been a single working mother, an entrepreneur, and one who is willing to take risks. Just recently she left the security and success of her native California for Denver to pursue her speaking and radio career fulltime.

As a strong supporter of working women, Judith sees one of her primary callings to instill hope in women as well as encouraging working women to strive for newer and higher levels of achievement.

"Women need to see other women as partners," Judith says. "Instead of comparing one another, I'd like to see more women reaching out a hand and saying, 'What can I do to help you along?'"

"Someone once helped me by sharing two hours of herself when I started in the book business. From that day on, I vowed that, I, too, would make it a point to give back to others what I had learned along the way."

Mary Whelchel is founder and speaker of the national radio program, "The Christian Working Woman," and owner/president of a consulting and training firm in a western suburb of Chicago.

Looking back on her career Mary admits, "I never planned to be a working woman, but I was forced into it—I was a divorced woman who had to support a child." Mary started her career as one of the first women in sales for IBM. From there she held a variety of management positions with other companies until doors opened eight years ago for her radio ministry.

The seed for this ministry was planted when Mary noticed the church she attended in Chicago offered no programs specifically designed for the needs of working women. "From that point," remembers Mary, "I started praying for direction and for one particular need I saw that wasn't being filled—no one on Christian radio ever talked about the working women.

"After eighteen months of praying, I received a call from a top Christian radio station in Chicago asking if I'd be a guest on a talk show. I knew the call was not a coincidence.

"After the show I presented my idea for a talk show for Christian working women to the host. Her response was overwhelmingly positive. With the help of several others, I put together a not-for-profit organization to fund the show and, in August 1984, we went on the air with one fifteen-minute weekly program."

Today, Mary's radio ministry is heard daily on more than four hundred stations across the country. Mary brings to her listeners, and to the readers of her popular "Women and Work" column in *Today's Christian Woman* magazine, sound biblical advice that is immensely practical and memorable. The stories and insights she shares convey a sincerity and understanding for the working woman you can't help but notice.

———◦◦———

Luci Swindoll, who recently retired as vice-president of public relations for Insight For Living in Anaheim, California, rounds out our group of contributors. Luci's career began more than thirty years ago in the corporate world with Mobil Oil Corporation. As a graduate with a commercial art degree, Luci joined Mobil as a draftsman with no intention of staying longer than a year. It was her plan to return to school to get a master's degree, but she liked her job so well she stayed. For many years she worked on art and illustrations for Mobil, ultimately finding herself in the field of rights of way and claims. At this point, she went to night school, studying brand new areas of learning: law, engineering, negotiating, and appraisal.

In 1984, Luci was promoted to manager of her department, which was responsible for negotiating contracts and agreements to lay pipeline in public and private property. On occasion, she was also called upon to settle disputes that might arise in these negotiations. She was the first woman to hold this executive position.

Now that she has retired (for a second time), Luci speaks across the nation approximately forty weekends a year and writes books. She has written eight and is trying to decide on the ninth: "I've got two or three burning topics floating around in my head," she says. "I'm not sure what's next."

A natural enthusiasm and love for life characterize Luci. "I'm not a workaholic," she readily admits. "I value a well-rounded life. The whole time I was with Mobil I always created time to play—I sang in the opera, I did art work on the side, I traveled. I am never content to be just one thing."

It is this enthusiasm and love of life that permeates Luci's advice for working women.

We encourage you to carve out a few minutes each day from your busy schedule to read a chapter or two of *The Workplace: Questions Women Ask*. We know you'll find Judith, Luci, and Mary a source of encouragement as you take to heart their words of wisdom and reassurance.

Louise A. Ferrebee and Marian V. Liautaud, Editors

Section 1

FITTING INTO THE WORKPLACE

By our very commitment to the Lord, Christian working women are supposed to bring different expectations, perspectives, and attitudes to the workplace. But, alas, we're human. And because of that reality, we many times find ourselves taking on the walk and talk of the world. We don't want to be perceived as "different." We so desperately want to fit in. And so we talk behind someone's back, or get caught up in hurtful gossip, or characterize co-workers as competitors rather than comrades.

Yet we are not called to be transformed by the marketplace but to transform the marketplace with the godly fruit of gentleness, kindness, patience, humility, compassion, and love. We are to be a breath of fresh air, a light to those around us.

Listen carefully, then, to what Luci, Judith, and Mary have to say about the benefits of *not* fitting in—and how you can keep your light shining brightly for all to see and enjoy.

Chapter 1

HOW DO I HANDLE THOSE TIMES I FEEL EXCLUDED FROM CO-WORKERS BECAUSE OF MY BELIEFS?
Judith Briles

e work and live in a world that stresses conformity. Consider the resume. Guaranteed, 99 percent of the college graduates who send one out this year will use buff-colored paper, start with their educational background, and end with "references available upon request."

While it might be prudent to adhere to convention as far as resumes are concerned, as Christians in the marketplace, there is no room for conformity when it comes to living out our beliefs. The Bible tells us we are here not to conform to the world but to follow Christ, which inevitably means there will be times when we feel excluded. Perhaps we must voice our displeasure at a lewd joke, or walk away from a gossip session—actions that say we aren't willing to be part of the gang at the expense of our Christian integrity.

A tension is certain to exist between us and our nonbelieving co-workers. But how do we get along successfully in the workplace without creating a "them versus us" attitude? How can we stand up for our convictions without alienating our co-workers?

A Different Challenge

First of all, we can remember our ultimate goal. James 4:4 says friendship with the world is not our goal but instead growing in the image of Christ. Because my base is Christ, I know that I don't have to be like everyone else.

Meeting in the Marketplace
What would you have said to Jesus when he befriended Zaccheus? No one else would talk to this man, yet Jesus called him out of the tree and went to dinner with him. Everyone said, 'How can Jesus have dinner with a sinner?' Jesus went where the sinners lived. He ate in their homes. We aren't going to ruin ourselves spiritually if we join a co-worker for dinner in a loud restaurant with people drinking at the bar. Like Jesus, in certain circumstances, we need to meet our co-workers where they are—that's what the marketplace is all about.

—Mary

When I started work as a stockbroker in the early seventies, I was one of only a few women in a male-dominated business. I heard comments like, "We know how she got the job." I was amazed by statements like this, but I think it fueled my determination to make sure my Christian witness came across consistently, from my attitude at work to the way I dressed. For instance, miniskirts were the rage, but I refused to wear them. I wanted my male counterparts to see me as a different kind of woman, someone who was willing to make a break from society's standards and live by a Christian code of conduct.

Part of maturing in our faith is learning that you don't have to talk and look like everybody else. It's not the easiest lesson to learn or practice, especially because we are conditioned by the world to view conformity as good. But I believe if you're not hurting anyone, if you are simply standing up for your beliefs—whether it is how you dress or act—go ahead and stand up with confidence. Jesus did.

Undoubtedly, there will be times when sticking with your convictions leaves you feeling more alone and less than confident. When you feel excluded ask yourself these questions to help keep you centered. Who do you want to be around? Who do you want as a role model? To whom do you want to be a role model? There is a great deal of truth in the old saying, "the company you keep is a reflection of who you are."

If you choose not to conform, people will notice you and, I think, begin to listen too. Once you have their attention, you need to be prepared to defend your beliefs and behavior. And remember, you will undermine your credibility if the work you produce is not first class. Make certain that if you do stand out because of your Christian convictions, everything about you shines. Otherwise, your choice not to conform in the office might be viewed as nothing more than petty idiosyncrasies.

Build No Walls

Everyone I worked with at Mobil knew I was a Christian but it wasn't something I flaunted. I didn't say, "Shape up. Put out your cigarettes. Quit telling dirty jokes." I wanted my co-workers to see my faith as one of the many factors that defined who I was. I never wanted to polarize myself from others and have them say, "She's a believer. What a drag. She's very legalistic and doesn't like the fact we do this and we do that." We can be and should try to be part of the team. Otherwise, we'll never have the opportunity to share our faith with the team.

—Luci

Choose Your Words Wisely

Time and again we'll come to a crossroad, a situation where we must make a choice—follow the crowd or take a stand. How can we express our beliefs in a nonjudgmental manner? The answer is in the words you choose. Sometimes if I get caught in a potentially compromising situation, I simply say, "That's not my style."

For instance, if after a conference some colleagues want to go to a noisy, smoke-filled bar, I'm comfortable saying, "That's not my style. I'd be glad to talk some more, but at a quieter restaurant."

Believe me, such an approach goes over much better than saying, "According to Ephesians 5:18, I can't go with you." How we phrase our personal beliefs significantly affects how our co-workers view us and accept us. If we come on with a holier-than-thou attitude, I guarantee you'll turn many away.

⋘⋙

If you do find yourself in the middle of a situation you find objectionable, like a gripe session about a co-worker or taking an extended coffee break, I encourage you to avoid making excuses for your behavior.

Instead of saying, "I can't stay and talk because I've got to . . . uh . . . get a report done," be honest and straightforward. Try something like, "It's okay if you want to talk about our boss like this, but I really feel uncomfortable. You'll have to excuse me." There is nothing wrong with expressing how you feel, as long as it isn't judgmental. I realize such a response takes courage, but the more often you do it, the easier it becomes.

Power of Silence

Some time ago, I turned on the TV and caught one of the popular afternoon talk shows. The host interviewed parents who had their young boys preaching on the school playground and on street corners. The kids would recite entire books of the Bible—they were incredible, like programmed computers. But I don't think they had a clue as to what they were preaching. Eventually the kids were considered disruptive at school and suspended.

That talk show made me think about how we as Christians operate in the workplace. Are we like those kids, loud and disruptive? The longer I'm in the business world, the more convinced I am that coming on too strong with our beliefs is the wrong approach.

If you hope to reach anyone at your office with the gospel, I would encourage you to use a "soft sell" approach. When I meet someone new, I try to figure her out. I share some of the ups and downs of my life. I use references and words that others can identify with. As I look at the Gospels, I see that gentleness and kindness were Jesus' method of working with others. He was kind toward the worst of the worst.

While your co-workers may not share your beliefs, be on the lookout for open dialogue. What can you share as a Christian? In your behavior and talk, what message are you giving out? If a lunch-table discussion turns into a tear-down session about another worker, why not add something positive about the person and derail the negative discussion?

Check Out the Environment

Without a doubt, some of us will work in environments that are anything but positive. It will be a daily battle to be a team player of the organization yet not conform to your co-workers' rules of the game. If you work for a company that in one way or another opposes your beliefs, realize there may always be a tension. That realization can help soften the times you feel labeled as different because of your beliefs.

Several years ago a publisher asked me to write a book for a company and then be their spokesperson as well. It was a significant contract, but before I could sign I had to know if the company was involved in the tobacco or alcohol business. I've seen the destruction such products cause and I wouldn't have felt comfortable representing such a company. The answer was no, so I proceeded to write the book, but added some lines that stated my personal convictions. The lines were edited out, but I stood firm. I asked for them to be reinstated and eventually they were. It was risky, but I was willing to lose the contract over the issue.

I don't believe that Christians are called to the workplace to be caped crusaders. We're called to do our job and do it well, not point out the bad guys and consider ourselves the good guys.

However, if the environment you're working in is so negative, if it is nearly impossible to withstand the pressures to conform to your co-workers, I strongly suggest you assess the situation. Ask yourself, Am I where I should be? Am I setting myself up for discrimination because my beliefs are so contrary to those of my co-workers? Am I in the wrong place?

If the answers are yes, then seriously consider moving on.

You may find yourself set up, excluded on purpose, and discriminated against because you made others feel uncomfortable. And when that happens, it's difficult to do your job well. I've found few people like to feel uncomfortable—they will go out of their way to make you look bad. You need to assess the situation realistically and determine if your workplace is the right fit.

A Sense of Hope

We've all had times when we'd like to toss in the towel. I remember when my son Frankie decided to quit school in first grade. I looked out the window and saw him and his friend Robin eating their lunches at the bus stop, closing their lunch boxes, then heading back home to announce their decision. I thought that was quite a big step for a first grader, but I told him life is long, it's hard, and it's not easy out there. I made him and his friend each another peanut-butter sandwich and told them to get back outside or they'd miss their bus. Just like Frankie, I've had moments I wanted to quit. But the bus came by and I got back on.

I put a lot of stock in the fact that God has placed us exactly where he wants us. It may be a tough situation. It may not be the most positive work environment. But our hope lies in knowing God is in control of the situation. He will lead us to be outspoken or to be quiet, to say yes or no. But be assured that we do have a purpose in where he has placed us.

At the end of the book tour for my book *The Confidence Factor*, I was scheduled to be on a show called "The Morning Exchange," in Cleveland, Ohio. The day before, tragedy had fallen—three young men had died after a high-school graduation party—the student body president, a star athlete, and the class valedictorian.

I was there to talk about confidence. How could I ignore this incredible crisis? As I was introduced, I immediately linked confidence to growing through crises and brought up the fact that my nineteen-year-old son had been killed five years ago. Although I was there to talk about *The Confidence Factor*, I felt it would be more appropriate to talk about overcoming tragedy and my book *When God Says No*.

Now keep in mind, I am on the number one morning show in Cleveland—not a religious station. The hosts went along with my redirection, the phone lines went crazy. After the segment, the producers asked if I would come back and do a full hour on their two-hour show. The emphasis—dealing with bad times, and definitely featuring *When God Says No* on the number one secular station!

Make It Happen

1. Have your friends serve as a sounding board for the times you feel excluded. Would they have handled the situation the same way you did? Have they been in similar circumstances? Have them help you see what God is doing in your life.

2. When the pressure to conform is great, or you're feeling like an outsider, consider a brief Bible study on Romans 8. How does Paul's advice apply to your present situation? Write out a verse that speaks to you, that gives you a clear sense of direction. Consider memorizing it and reciting it at the beginning of each workday.

3. Keep your eyes on Jesus—read your Bible daily, make time for a Bible-study group, and continue to refresh your memory with what he has to say about being in this world as a light to others. After a particularly hard day at work, be bold in your prayers and ask the Lord to offer you insights from his Word that will keep you going.

Chapter 2

COULD AN OFFICE AFFAIR REALLY HAPPEN TO ME?
Mary Whelchel

ot long ago, I received a letter from a Christian woman who said she had fallen in love with a married man at work. She knew it was wrong and felt miserable beyond words. In fact, she talked about taking her own life. I was amazed she was considering something that desperate, yet she wasn't willing to end the affair. Her letter isn't the only one I've received that details this type of situation. Others have written me about similar experiences. The details might be different, but one common thread remains the same: none of these women ever thought an affair could happen to them.

I don't want to paint a gloom and doom picture regarding male/female relationships on the job. I've worked with many men over the years and have enjoyed positive friendships with them. But, unfortunately, we work in a world where extramarital relationships are common and tolerated, to a certain degree. I believe our senses have become dulled to the very real dangers of illicit affairs. For this reason, I encourage every woman to think through very carefully what her own code of conduct will be—a set of guidelines that won't be compromised. In doing so we will be preparing ourselves to face temptation before it happens.

Each of us is vulnerable sexually, so it's important to have standards set up ahead of time to avoid the snare of an office affair.

Play No Favorites

One way I avoided potential problems with male/female friendships was to make certain I included everyone in my group—I made it a point not to play favorites. Also, I always presented myself as a professional, serious about her job responsibilities yet at the same time friendly and fun to work with.

—Luci

A good place to start is to understand that men and women think and react differently. To generalize for a moment, when men make a decision they tend to base it on fact. When women make a decision, they often put a lot of stock in their emotions. Granted, it's not always this black and white. And it doesn't mean women can't think rationally and logically and men don't have emotions. But we need to recognize that male and female thought processes are different. If we don't acknowledge these differences we're vulnerable to misinterpretation and misunderstandings with our male co-workers.

Because women are often more sensitive and relational, we tend to view our co-workers—men and women—as individuals we want to get to know better. We want to know what's happening in their lives. We want to be a friend, a confidant. These are wonderful traits God has given to us. But at the same time, we must realize they can make us vulnerable. A relationship with a male co-worker can easily become too friendly.

Therefore, I suggest a vital guideline: although we can have friendships with men, for appearance's sake, and as an extra precaution, be reserved about what you share. Don't be as open as you might be with a woman. Realize there are certain things that are better left unsaid.

Your personal life—your marriage or, if you're a single woman, your private struggles, are not the kinds of things you want to share with a male co-worker—no matter how understanding and helpful he may be. For example, if there are certain things missing in your marriage—say it's not as exciting as it was in earlier years or your husband doesn't talk much—and you start discussing this with a male friend, he can begin to feed your ego and fill in the missing pieces in your life. That's how affairs often begin.

Comments like, "You look nice today," "You did a great job on that report," or "That hair style is very becoming to you," add up, especially if you're not getting affirmation from others. They feel good. You begin to warm up to this person, to open up and soon divulge a little more about yourself. Before long, a friend can become a confidant, and a confidant can become a lover. The door is now opened to that possibility.

It's also important to realize that women can sometimes

Keep Talking

When both husband and wife are busy professionals, it's easy to grow apart despite the fact you live in the same house and see each other every day. If you don't take time to communicate—really talk about the issues—you can become total strangers. There would be fewer office affairs and divorces if couples would just talk. My husband and I have made it a priority to talk every day about what's going on in our lives and how we feel about the events of the day.

—Judith

read more into a man's comments than he intends. Your co-worker may be saying complimentary things merely as a courtesy with no ulterior motive. Words carry a lot of power and it's easy to assume there are hidden meanings between the lines.

———

Along with not sharing too much about your own personal life is the practice of not inquiring into your male co-workers' personal lives either. I make it a point never to talk with a man about his marriage unless it is in positive terms. I purposefully watch out for those sad stories about relationships—I'm not the one who should be counseling a male co-worker about his marriage. If you catch yourself saying, "I'm really sorry to hear you and your wife are having troubles," that's like giving him a free shoulder to cry on. It's a dangerous path to start down.

I tried to get to know the wives of the men I worked closely with. By becoming friends, they knew I was not a threat to their marriage. And then when conversations with co-workers did cross over into their personal lives, we could focus on their wives and families.

This tactic proved valuable with one of my managers, who sometimes seemed to want our relationship to go beyond professional boundaries. I remember talking about his wife and his kids every chance I had. She was a successful woman so I could easily point out the terrific things she did, or how I admired her.

He knew from my conversations, which often alluded to my respect for his wife and family, that there was no chance of anything ever happening between us.

Check Your Messages

I was one of the first women to hold a sales position with IBM at a time when companies were not accustomed to having a female sales representative. My manager told me, "Mary, you're going to get lots of passes. You need to be prepared."

I fully expected to fight men off on a daily basis. Yet it didn't happen. One day as my boss and I made sales calls together, I jokingly said, "I've been selling about six months now, and I don't think anybody's made a pass at me yet. What's wrong with me?"

His response was memorable. He said, "When you go into a customer's office, it's obvious you are there to sell him IBM products. You are all business—it's written all over you. The message you send out is 'don't waste your time.' "

I learned then that our body language, the way we dress, and what we talk about are all messages we need to take into account in the office. What are your nonverbal messages saying to your male co-workers?

————

Entertaining is another area where it's wise to set guidelines. Although I have never had a hard-and-fast rule about not having a one-on-one lunch or dinner with a businessman, I try to avoid it when possible. There is always the potential that such a business meeting would be troublesome for a co-worker's spouse, or be a stumbling block for a co-worker who isn't as strong. Set some guidelines for yourself that you feel comfortable with when it comes to luncheons, dinners, or business travel. If a situation would be at all questionable or if you feel uncomfortable, look for some suitable alternatives. For example, try to take another co-worker along, if possible, or suggest an on-site meal in the company facility, if one is available.

If alternative suggestions are not working, you don't need to be embarrassed to say something like, "I think it would be better if we discussed this situation in the conference room." You don't have to give reasons, but if pressed, you have every right to let that male co-worker know you're uncomfortable with how it might look to others.

It's All in Your Head

Affairs don't necessarily have to be physical. A very subtle, but nonetheless dangerous kind of involvement is to be mentally or emotionally devoted to a male co-worker.

I remember a married woman once confided in me that a woman who worked with her husband had stolen him from her—even though there was not a physical affair. At the office, this woman would fulfill his need for conversation. They shared a job and had a great deal in common. He found the office contact enjoyable, and when he came home at night he didn't feel like sharing his day or his struggles with his wife. His need for companionship was being met by his female co-worker.

The office is an artificial environment. We usually are on our best behavior. Work hours are our prime time when we're alert and creative. And we usually try to look sharp. Our co-workers see the best side of us and we see the best side of them. Remember, the person you know at work is likely a different person a home.

A danger signal is when you find thoughts of your co-worker lingering in your mind after hours. You daydream about him, recalling something complimentary he said. Women are good at this. Consider it a warning when you start trying to please a co-worker or impress him with your looks or your work, in hopes of gaining his affirmation.

Move Quickly

If you do find yourself attracted to another man other than your husband, or if you're single and you're attracted to a co-worker who is married or a nonbeliever, move fast.

Seldom are people able to walk away from a relationship once they've taken the first step or two. Maybe nothing more has happened than a few conversations, a long lunch, or quiet dinner. But then they realize they have feelings for one another. Very few people back out at that point. Very few.

Ask for a transfer to another department. Consider finding a new job. If that's not possible, see that your paths don't cross unless absolutely necessary. Nothing is too drastic to prevent you from giving in to your temptation. In many cases, your marriage, which is of eternal significance to God, could be at stake. Before you get hooked, do something.

I'm sure that some of you reading this now find yourselves already two or three steps down the pathway toward an involvement with a male co-worker. It's not too late to turn back, no matter how far you've gone. Jesus told us to take drastic steps—cut off our hands or gouge out our eyes—to avoid temptation.

Don't be afraid to confront that male co-worker and say, "I'm concerned about the tone of our relationship. I feel it necessary to limit our interactions to business dealings only." State how you feel, and then exit. Don't begin to compromise or work on negotiations.

As difficult as you may think it is to cut off a relationship that feels good and meets some of your needs for companionship and acceptance, the pain you are going to deal with later if you allow this relationship to develop into an affair is greater than anything you can imagine. The earlier you turn around and head in the right direction, the easier it is to untangle yourself.

Dropping our standards can happen subtly. I know from personal experience. In the ten years I wasn't walking with the Lord and was in the corporate world, I found myself in several compromising situations. More often than not I had moved to that point slowly, not in one big jump. Looking back I realize I let down one standard, then another, and another until finally I'd wonder, How did I let that happen?

Accountability to another Christian is one solid way to keep your standards from slipping. Early on, find a close, nonjudgmental friend, preferably someone outside of work, and say, "I'm feeling weak here," or, "I can see trouble coming. Help keep me true to my principles. Call me up. Make sure I'm not falling in knee deep."

A short time ago a young man at the church I attend introduced himself to me. He had listened to several of my radio broadcasts and wanted to know if I had any literature for his girlfriend, a nonbeliever.

We talked for a little bit and then I looked him straight in the eye and said, "You're getting really involved with this young woman. You're on dangerous ground."

He replied, "I realize that."

I said, "You know, once your heart gets involved you can't control it. Who are you accountable to?"

He had another friend standing there, so I said, "Are you going to hold him accountable? What if he goes too far? What if he marries a nonbeliever?"

When it comes to relationships, accountability is extremely important. But we don't like accountability as a rule, especially when it involves relationships, because they feel good. And when they bring excitement or happiness to our life, it's hard to confront the truth about them.

Rather than confront our feelings, we go into denial. I've heard women say, "I can handle this. It won't go any further. It will just stay in my mind."

At this point, though, you're already in trouble.

Matthew 5:28 reminds us, "Anyone who looks at a woman lustfully has already committed adultery with her in his heart." What we think is what we are. Our thought life directs and controls us. We have to ask ourselves daily, What am I putting into my mind?

It is essential to set your principles for male/female relationships on the job from day one. You can't learn to swim in a storm. So anticipate temptation in the workplace and set your standards ahead of time. In fact, err on the side of caution and set stricter guidelines than you think you need, because once you think you can trust yourself, you're in trouble.

I don't trust myself, even to this day. Although I'm not exposed to the corporate environment to the degree I once was, I know that I can still be attracted and vulnerable given the right (or wrong) set of circumstances. I know my flesh, and I know I've got to set strong guidelines clearly stamped, "I will not cross this line."

And once I have those guidelines firmly in place, then I can be free to enjoy many professional and rewarding friendships with my male colleagues.

Can Men and Women Be "Just Friends"?
Elizabeth Cody Newenhuyse

Working side by side each day, friendships are certain to develop among your female, as well as male, co-workers. Here's how to keep your friendships with your male co-workers positive.

If you are married, make sure your husband knows this friend. Whether it is a co-worker, professional acquaintance, old college friend, or acquaintance from church, introduce your husband to him. Talk about your husband (and children) with the friend. Turn the "exclusive friend" into the "family friend."

Be careful of too much time alone with the same male friend. My personal preference—not a hard-and-fast rule, but a preference—is to mix with male friends in the context of groups or couple friendships. Obviously there will be exceptions, and much of this is a matter of degree. But the time-alone-together factor bears monitoring.

Have a good reason for your friendships with other men—especially if either one of you is married. Again, and this is admittedly a personal bias, I would not be comfortable with a "stand-alone" male friendship, the way I am friends with women, simply because we enjoy each other. In other words, my friendships with men are almost all based on a common interest or other shared connection: work, church, and so on. I would feel uneasy about actively seeking out another man: "Let's go out for breakfast!" But if there were a *reason* to meet for breakfast—and I felt absolutely safe about the relationship—I would not hesitate to make the appointment.

Know what kind of man you find attractive. As my friend Eileen said, she finds her friend Mike attractive, and therefore takes extra care in her relationship with him. And "attractive" is not limited to physical appearance. This is the very subtle danger in male/female friendships: the stronger the friendship, or the more you have in common with a husband of a girlfriend or married co-worker, the faster the red flags need to go up. Most women respond most strongly to an *emotional* connection, not a sexual one. If you—or your friend—are married, reserve those close emotional connections for your spouses.

Look to the state of your own marriage. Sometimes another man might seem more companionable, sympathetic, or stimulating than your husband. Certainly your spouse cannot and should not be all things to you. However, if you are feeling an inappropriate delight in another man's attention, you need to evaluate the state of your communication and intimacy with your husband. Talk to your spouse; express your needs. You may be surprised to find that he's been feeling the same way.

Pray for discernment. We shouldn't struggle with temptation alone, and we don't have to. God wants us to turn our friendships over to him, to ask him for wisdom and discernment in all things. We should, of course, pray regularly about and for all our friends. But we need to ask God for special guidance in our friendships with the opposite sex—that he help us keep them healthy, pure, and pleasing to him.

A good friendship is a great gift, not easily found. It *is* possible to maintain wholesome friendships with men. But as you do, remember what is a much greater gift: your integrity.

From Today's Christian Woman
(September/October 1990)

Handling Sexual Harassment
Sally Lawrence

Sexual harassment can and does happen, even in good companies. By definition, sexual harassment is unwelcome sexual conduct that interferes with your performance or creates an intimidating, hostile, or offensive work environment. Here are some tips for handling this tough situation.

• Don't kid yourself into thinking it's going to get better. Sexual harassment may start out innocently—placing a hand on your shoulder, leaning too far into your personal space, or admiring your jewelry—but your harasser will only grow more bold in his advances. Even if the situation cools off, be on guard for a repeat performance.

• Don't expect your harasser to stop on his own. Confront your harasser's improper behavior right away. Let the harasser know you won't stand for his jokes or advances. Report the situation to a supervisor. If your harasser *is* the supervisor, appeal to the next level of management or personnel. Doing nothing sends a subtle message—either you're too weak to stand up for yourself or you're a prime target for involvement.

• Don't put yourself in a vulnerable situation. Refuse his lunch invitations. Make plans to go out with your co-workers. Try not to come in too early or stay after others have left for the day. Leave your door open.

• Don't carry the burden alone. Tell a trusted friend or co-worker. You may discover that you're not the only one who has dealt with harassment in your department.

• Don't value your job above your marriage or emotional stability. Ask yourself what's really important. If you must resign to avoid a volatile situation, believe that God will honor your decision. Regardless of the outcome, you can appeal to God to protect and provide for you.

From Today's Christian Woman
(January/February 1991)

Make It Happen

1. Confess a fantasy affair to the Lord. Admit your weakness over the situation. Then have a sentence prayer like, "Lord, help me to keep my thoughts pure that they will bring glory to you." Use it the moment your mind starts to wander into the danger zone.

2. Consider writing your guiding principles for working with men on paper—ones that will prevent you from stepping over the line. Often writing something down makes it concrete and forces us to clearly think through how we will handle a situation.

3. Periodically assess your friendships with male co-workers. Have you been too open? Have they been sharing too much of their personal lives? If you're married, ask yourself if you'd be happy with your husband having the same level of friendship with a female co-worker.

Chapter 3

HOW CAN I BE A FRIEND TO A CO-WORKER I FIND OFFENSIVE?
Mary Whelchel

friend of mine is a very conservative, structured Christian woman. At one time, she worked for a major Chicago law firm—a business that matched her clean-cut, reserved style. One day, a new woman joined the office staff who was the extreme opposite of my friend. The newcomer's clothes, music, make-up, and hair style were eccentric—almost a nineties version of a hippie. Immediately, both women did a mental assessment, *We have nothing in common.* My friend thought to herself, *I won't bother talking with her more than necessary.*

At Christmas time, my friend brought a nativity scene to work thinking it would be a good way to keep the focus of the season on Christ and possibly witness to others in the office. Not long after she arranged the nativity scene on the corner of her desk, the new co-worker stopped by to admire it. The two struck up a conversation and soon my friend discovered her "hippie" co-worker was an intelligent and intriguing woman.

They went out for lunch several times and my friend was surprised to find she really liked this co-worker. "She's interesting," I remember her telling me. "Of course there are things about her I could never accept, but once I looked past the hair and the clothes, I found a nice person who had something to say."

These two women became friends—amiable co-workers who no longer purposefully avoided each other. Had my friend insisted on operating under the opinion, "You don't fit my mold, so I won't talk to you," those communication lines never would have opened up.

Opening the Lines

Often, people who are offensive have something inside that is eating at them. They have no peace. When we create a climate for them to find peace in our sphere of influence, they usually calm down. Sometimes the offensive party will then talk about what is troubling them, and with communication comes healing.

—*Luci*

Like my friend, we all make instant assessments of a co-worker who doesn't match our style. We tend to shut out others we find offensive. But what we need to realize is that we are put in the workplace as salt and light. Our co-workers are not in our life by accident. We are put together to touch one another's lives in unique ways. Yet few Christians see it that way.

I wish I could show you the letters I receive from women who say, "I can't stand the dog-eat-dog environment. If only I could work for a Christian organization." Their definition of a perfect work environment is working only with Christians.

Christian organizations are essential. But if we all cloistered together in the safety of a Christian working environment, we would never reach the world. We need to shed the mind-set of wanting to be separated from those who are different.

So how do we get along with a co-worker we find offensive or irritating, or who leads a life in direct contradiction to biblical principles and doesn't deserve our respect?

Tune into God

I've found the first step in getting along with co-workers who challenge me is to turn to the Bible and tune into God daily. We need to bring before the Lord all those relationships we find difficult and ask for his help in reaching our goal—to let Jesus love people through us.

Now I admit, there are a lot of people I don't want to love, that I can't love. But a firsthand experience I had several years ago showed me that Jesus can indeed love the unlovable through me. I am not alone in my struggle.

At one point in my career I worked for an alcoholic—a man who really made my stomach turn. I didn't like John (not his real name) at all—his lifestyle, his mannerisms, his style of management. I remember one night thinking about him in a very derogatory way. And just as though God were sitting there beside me, he said, "I love John as much as I love you."

> ## Friendly, Not Friends
> *It's a fallacy to think we have to be a friend to everyone we meet. We don't. However, be friendly, ask about a co-worker's day, say "hello." Most of us are brought up to believe everyone is our friend. Unfortunately, they are not—not everyone is friend material.*
> *—Judith*

The thought hit me like a bolt of lightning. *God loves John as much as he loves me?* Believe it or not, it had never dawned on me that God loved those people I found so distasteful as much as he loved me. Jesus died for my co-workers just as he died for me. I had been taught that truth my whole life. But until that moment, I had not truly grasped what it meant. After that conversation with God, my approach toward John changed.

When I can look at my co-workers the way God looks at them, I see they are not all that hard to love. Once God gives me the ability to love, it's my job to live out 1 Corinthians 13:4-8—to show the actions of love each day in the workplace.

Those co-workers who look so objectionable to us—who might practice a homosexual lifestyle, who cheat, or think nothing of sexual promiscuity—are loved by God. They are savable.

Before you march into work tomorrow, determined to be a friend to all, I offer a word of wisdom. We need to remember that we don't make friends in the workplace solely for the purpose of witnessing. We make friends because that is what Jesus would do and because we care. The love of Jesus in us says to others, "I care about you personally. Jesus died for you. I'd love to be able to share Jesus with you. I hope someday you'll come to the Lord, but that's not why I'm making friends with you."

We hear a lot about lifestyle evangelism—developing relationships with others and building trust as a prelude to openly sharing the Gospel. I believe such an approach is valid, but we must watch ourselves and our motives. Our goal is not to befriend a co-worker so we can railroad them into the Kingdom.

Make the Move

I've found one thing that often prevents us from moving beyond our comfort zone and reaching out to others is fear. Fear of the unknown, fear that we'll feel uncomfortable and awkward with nothing to say, or fear we will somehow damage our Christian testimony. But we need to overcome those fears and take that first step. Like my friend who worked at the law firm, we have to put aside our reservations and open the door to conversation.

I'll be honest, at times in my life I've avoided friendships for fear I might not know what to say or it would appear I condoned my co-workers' questionable behavior. Years ago my daughter Julie and I lived in a condominium in the city. Across the hall was a couple living together. I wanted to be certain that Julie understood their arrangement was not biblically acceptable, but I also wanted to befriend them, for they were delightful people. Gradually, we got to know them. We enjoyed each other's company and my daughter wasn't confused by our friendship. She understood that we could be friends without condoning their lifestyle.

One evening, when my neighbor's friend was away on business, she and I went out for dinner. She opened up and shared her concerns—and I was surprised to find that behind this "I've got it all together" facade was a confused woman who needed my compassion and friendship. Often we best communicate what Jesus is like by our actions better than our words.

———————

More than likely, we'll run into situations in the workplace when we'll wonder what others will think when we associate with those so opposite of us. Whenever you feel that way, I would remind you that we don't have to approve of everything a person does in order to be a friend.

Jesus frequently associated with sinners. He went out of his way to build relationships with people whom no one else would associate with. That tells us something. Zaccheus, Matthew, the woman caught in adultery, the Samaritan woman—he treated each one with gentleness, kindness, and respect.

Does that mean he approved of the woman having five husbands? No. Or committing adultery? Of course not. But everybody is loved by God and has potential. You never know the possibilities within that co-worker who gossips, who constantly makes sexual innuendoes, or who treats others rudely.

Consider the story of the Samaritan woman in John 4. Jesus spoke to her at the well, and soon after she became a witness and told the whole town about Jesus. Who would have ever guessed this woman would be used by God? We would have all turned our backs on her and said she's unworthy. The disciples thought it was absolutely incredible that Jesus would talk to her. Yet Jesus knew that despite this woman's background and actions, there was a heart that was open and receptive.

So often the one we least think will be receptive to what we have to share may indeed be the one who is searching for truth. When we start making judgments we can miss a lot of good opportunities.

Building Tolerance

One fruit of the Spirit is described in Colossians 3:13 as bearing with each other. In other words, being tolerant of one another. Many Christians, me included, have little tolerance for those we find offensive. I admit I'll look at someone, and if they don't measure up lifestyle-wise, I start to bristle. Intolerance often seems to be a natural response. We wonder if accepting another's behavior will cause us to compromise our standards or our testimony.

Thankfully, the answer is no. As you befriend co-workers who are offensive, whose morals are in direct contrast to yours, you can do so while holding tight to biblical principles. If you're being a friend, talking to someone, and caring about them, you're well within biblical guidelines. Keep those relationships at the top of your prayer list, and I believe the Lord will let you know where to draw the line or when spending time with a nonbeliever is bringing you down to his level.

Tolerance is not the same as compromise, and it's something we need to pray for daily. I often remind myself that even when people are not where they are supposed to be, Christian or non-Christian, I can continue to love them and associate with them. I can tolerate their behavior, which may not be up to standard, simply because I am a Christian and I hang in there longer. I also remind myself that while they might not be everything they should be, neither am I.

One of the greatest benefits of having spent ten years away from the Lord (if you can call them benefits) is that I can remember those years when my lifestyle was below par. I wonder what would have happened to me if my friends hadn't kept loving me and praying for me? I knew my friends didn't approve of my lifestyle choices, yet they didn't disown me, they didn't forsake me, or preach to me. Instead, they hung in there with me and prayed for me.

Even though I've been on both sides of the fence, a non-practicing believer and now in Christian ministry, I still find myself prone to self-righteous thinking when it comes to others. Whenever I start thinking others are too difficult or irritating to deal with, I look at what God has done in my life.

I remember how tolerant and patient he was with me. I

literally had to reach a point where I was at the end of my rope spiritually before I would even listen to what God was saying to me. I'm a slow learner—it took a decade for me to listen, but God persisted. I need to have the same patience and persistence with my co-workers. I may never see the results of my efforts during my time with a co-worker, but that is not reason to give up.

My hope is that more marketplace Christians will see the work world as their mission field—a place to practice tolerance and show love to those whose lifestyles and behaviors are anything but Christian.

Now that I'm doing business seminars, I don't touch people's lives day after day like I once did. I touch them one day, then leave, never to see them again. I don't have the luxury of building relationships like I used to, and sometimes I almost feel left out because that's where you impact someone's life—being with them day after day after day. The work world gives us these unique opportunities.

I heard a minister challenge his teenagers to pick out a fellow student at school least likely to accept Christ and then start praying for that person constantly. One of his kids picked a boy with spiked green hair and an earring. He continued to pray for an opportunity to make friends with this boy, and over time this boy came to church with him and accepted Christ.

Wouldn't it be great if we entered the marketplace like this, saying, "Lord, I don't think this person will ever accept you but I'm going to do anything I can to be her friend. I'm going to try to get to know this person, and then I'm going to pray." Think of what could happen. I challenge you to try this.

I have a friend who has the ability to see every person she meets as an individual, specially created by God. No matter who she talks to, whether it's a clerk or a gas station attendant, she touches peoples' lives. Her eyes tell you she cares, even if you just talk to her for a minute.

She enjoys people—that's her gift. We could all use a little of this gift as we look at our co-workers and say, "I want to be a friend. You're important because God loves you."

Make It Happen

1. Pick the least likely person in your company that you'd ever talk to or be friends with. Begin to pray for this person and your relationship daily. Note when and how God leads you together. Could you have done it on your own? Have you been able to overcome those intolerances that previously separated you?

2. Bring the toughest work relationship you have before the Lord. Ask him to help you explore all of your hidden feelings and concerns about this relationship. Ask that he help you get to the core of why you feel this way about your co-worker. Could this person exhibit behavior you see in yourself and dislike? Once you know why you feel as you do, ask for God's help in developing a new attitude that will make Jesus' love real to this co-worker.

3. Look up several translations of 1 Corinthians 13:4-8. Read each for a greater understanding of what love should be. Select the translation that best speaks to you, then consider memorizing it. Recite it during those moments at work when you're tempted not to show love to a co-worker.

Chapter 4

HOW CAN I DISTINGUISH OFFICE GOSSIP FROM COMPANY GRAPEVINE INFORMATION I NEED TO KNOW?

Judith Briles

t a governmental agency in West Virginia, employees are not allowed to smoke in any of the buildings. If you want to smoke, you've got to visit one of several small smoking huts spread throughout the acreage. When I visited this company late last spring, I noticed everyone, smokers *and* nonsmokers alike, gravitated to these huts—from the CEO down to the floor sweeper. Why? Because, if they wanted to know what was going on in the agency, those little huts were the place to be.

Though it was amusing, I was amazed at the lengths people would go to be part of the agency grapevine. Yet, aren't we all a little like the West Virginia staff when it comes to wanting to know the ins and outs of the company we work for? As Christians, though, we're sensitive to the dangers of gossip, so we sometimes wonder, Is the grapevine the same as gossip?

Not necessarily.

When I was a stockbroker, there was a man named Dennis, who, every three months, would come in and sell his three shares of stock from the computer company he worked for. And I would always ask him, "How are things going?"

"Oh, really slow, Judith," he'd say. "We haven't been very busy." Dennis worked in shipping at the company headquarters just up the street from my office. Immediately, his casual remark signaled to me that business had slowed down there. Orders were not coming in and shipments were not going out, therefore, earnings would also be going down. As a stockbroker, information like that was invaluable to my job.

And that is the distinction between gossip and grapevine information. In general, grapevine information should help you do your job better, and above all, it should be based on fact, not rumor.

Every Little Bit Counts

While you might have a very small outreach, it's going to make a difference to someone. Co-workers begin to notice the little things that make you stand out—like knowing when to talk, when to keep your mouth shut, and how to retain another's confidences. As these little things add up you will have a greater and greater affect as a Christian in the workplace.

—Luci

Passing the Grapes

The company grapevine can keep us up-to-date on movements or changes within a business—changes that could translate into missed opportunities or a wrong career move on our part if we don't know about them.

Take, for instance, the development of a new product line. Let's say you learn the company plans to devote significant time and energy to the new product, which means the struggling product you've been working on will move to a slower track. Though your immediate situation may be sidetracked, if you keep abreast of what's happening you might spot a new opportunity. Maybe you have some ideas or experience that could play into the new product. Armed with your inside information, you can approach the right person with your ideas and suddenly you're a player in this new venture, someone management might not even have considered. The company benefits and so do you, with new responsibilities and added value on the job.

Another reason it pays to keep your ear to the grapevine is it can reduce the stress that comes from uncertainty. As you listen to talk, you can learn if your company's situation is good or bad, if a new product line directly related to your work is about to go under, or if layoffs are imminent and you need to polish up your resume.

As your responsibilities within a company increase so does your need to tap into the grapevine. If you've moved to a point where you "birth" your own projects, your work becomes a greater reflection of who you

Pop In the Positives
Whenever you hear something negative about management or a co-worker, follow it up with something positive. This at least allows you to bring some balance to the discussion as well as what is entering your mind.
—Mary

are. And naturally, if your reputation is at stake, you want to do all you can to see your "baby" succeed. So tap into that grapevine—listen to your supervisor and management above. And don't discount those below you who are often privy to vital company insights. Remember the smoking hut—everyone dropped in!

As you hear information about the company, check out its credibility. Did someone you trust tell you this information? Will what you've learned help you perform better as an employee? If so, then act on the information. Know it's okay to participate in the discussion, but remember to keep it to the facts.

However, listen carefully. If any of what you hear has a malicious tone to it or the taint of a rumor, without any fact to support it, shy away from it. Grapevine information should help you do your job better, keep you sharp for opportunities, or help you better understand why certain decisions were made by management.

Words as Weapons

At times, the line can blur between valuable grapevine information and gossip. As Christians we need to be aware that gossip does happen in all companies and we are not immune to it.

Just look at how we respond to the soap operas on television. If we miss one episode, we'll ask a friend, "So what did Joan do when Bob found out?" People like to talk about people. After all, gossip is entertaining. But it's equally destructive.

Several years ago I saw gossip destroy the integrity of a dear Christian friend—a fine mother and community volunteer. As a result of her strong involvement and concern for our town, my friend was encouraged to run for local office and, in fact, was elected mayor. Not long before her first meeting with the town council, she received a call from a woman who had strongly supported her throughout the campaign. The woman said, "When you get your council package, give me a call and I'll come over and tell you how to vote." My friend politely said, "Nobody tells me how to vote, however, I do welcome your input."

The woman was incensed at her reply and began a subtle gossip campaign that destroyed my friend's credibility. It even got to the point of criminal charges against my friend—all of which were proven false, but not until my friend had poured thousands of dollars into defending her name. Even though the charges were dropped, everyone paid a high price for one spiteful person's rumors. My friend's family was deeply hurt, so the community lost a valued family when they decided to move away, and the county spent unnecessary money prosecuting a case that had no foundation.

Granted, not all gossip goes to this extreme, but it's potential for destruction is almost limitless. And as Christians in the work force we need to set a standard—neither will we encourage gossip nor tolerate it.

Beating the Office Buzz

While it sounds simple, I've found the best way to combat the tendency to gossip is simply to not do it. Recently, I was a guest speaker for a large woman's group on a cruise. One evening, several of us got together to socialize. One woman began making fun of another member of our group who wasn't with us. Admittedly, this other woman was a little odd, but it wasn't right for us to talk about her behind her back.

"This makes me uncomfortable, I don't want to hear this," I said. "If you want me to stay let's talk about something different. This isn't okay with me, and I'll leave if it continues."

My comment changed the whole tone of the conversation, and I was able to stay. It might feel awkward, but as Christians we need to speak out and say, "I'm not going to participate." If the discussion turns to someone's behavior or sharing information about a person without her knowledge or permission, it's best to either excuse yourself immediately or express your feelings about the way the conversation is moving. While it might seem scary at first, especially if it's a co-worker or your supervisor you have to speak up to, stand firm. If you continually refuse to engage in gossip, others will soon learn this is what your personal integrity dictates.

Oftentimes we share information either because we are asked a question or we're concerned about another person. Be in tune with how you interact with your co-workers, how you divulge information.

Let's say you have knowledge that a co-worker's behavior could somehow be destructive to a project you're working on, and it's interfering with your ability to do the job. I don't think it's gossip to go to somebody above you and say, "I'm concerned about Marge. I've noticed a change in her behavior that worries me. It appears to be affecting her work and I think you need to talk to her."

When you're considering sharing something you've heard about a co-worker, before you even open your mouth ask yourself: Why am I telling this? What's the purpose? What's the benefit? Who does this help? Who can this hurt?

If what you say has the potential to hurt someone or alter another's perception of this person, why are you doing it? Learn to think of the end result of your words.

As Christian working women, we have the ability to model Christ in the workplace. And that includes how we treat others with our words. Gossip is fun and tempting but it's also like throwing leaves into the air. As the wind catches them, they scatter all over. Yet what if you find out your words were wrong? Your co-worker really didn't do or say what you told others. You want to go back and gather up all those leaves, but you can't—it's impossible. Your words are out there forever.

Another key to avoiding gossip is pinpointing where in the company it most often occurs. I've found that quite often gossip flourishes in large, open work areas. Cafeterias and lunch rooms can be hot spots. Also, since women tend to talk more than men, gossip seems to be more prevalent in female-dominated businesses. Be aware of your environment. Tune into where gossip happens, and if you're easily tempted by gossip, consider avoiding those areas.

While we need to show Christ's love to our co-workers, we also need to be wise about whom we choose as friends. Office mates don't always make the best confidants. As women, I think we have a tendency to divulge personal details to a female co-worker just because she's a woman—not because she can keep a confidence or truly cares for us. It's wise to expand our friendships but at the same time realize that too much familiarity can be a breeding ground for gossip. Be discerning when you entrust personal information to someone.

A Word about Cliques

In almost any setting cliques can occur, and the workplace is no exception. Taking coffee breaks or having lunch with the same set of women can be a positive aspect of your job. It can also be detrimental. It all depends on what comes out of the group.

I get together regularly with a group of women and we can talk nonstop for hours. But we make it a point to talk about issues and concerns, not people. One time I needed their feedback on a show I was doing about domestic violence. Another time we had an interesting discussion on what feminism really meant. Those times together proved to be intellectually stimulating. So, before you pass judgment on a clique, ask yourself, What is it accomplishing? Is there good coming from our time together? What are the benefits, if any, of being in that group of co-workers?

If the clique only generates gossip, don't be concerned about being on the outside. Know that the clique is not where Christ wants you to walk.

It takes discernment to determine if what you're hearing is legitimate grapevine information or just plain gossip. Keep your ears and eyes open. If you take care in what you say to others and ask the Lord for wisdom in using information you hear, you will be able to distinguish between the two.

"She Did What?"
Jane J. Struck

We may not have the strength to create worlds, but the Bible tells us our words *do* have power over others; power to crush, or power to nurture; power to curse, or power to praise. While it's a constant struggle, I've found asking certain questions helps me battle gossip.

Is it really necessary to reveal this detail about my friend/acquaintance? A friend of mine laughingly says, "If we can't gossip, what's left to talk about?" It's true—because we are so relationally-oriented, other people and their actions make up the bulk of our conversations. Life would be pretty dull if all we talked about were budget deficits, political unrest, or recycling. But we cross the fine line between sharing a prayer concern and gossiping when we start focusing on unnecessary or confidential details. It's okay—even biblical—to shoulder someone else's burdens through prayer, and sometimes that means those concerns get discussed openly. However, as my sister-in-law Terry, a nurse whose job demands confidentiality, observed, "When I talk about others for the purpose of sharing prayer requests, I only say what I know is true and what will not damage their reputation." Certain facts may be true; certain problems may exist; but if it's potentially damaging to elaborate on them, or if it violates a confidence, stop before you speak.

How would my friend/acquaintance feel if she knew what I was saying about her? Christ's call for us to treat others as we'd like to be treated applies to our words as well as our actions. It helps me to stop and put myself in the shoes of the person I'm talking about.

How would I feel if the person I talked about heard my words? Conventional wisdom teaches, "Don't say anything about someone you wouldn't want to say to her face." How difficult it is for me to apply that to my daily speech! Yet from time to time I've envisioned every hypocritical thought I have entertained, every catty word I have said, replayed on a giant movie screen in heaven. There will be no hiding then. This thought is so sobering it makes me reassess how I'm talking about others. It vividly reminds me of how often I say things I'd never want people to know I've said—because I think I can get away with it.

Why am I really gossiping about this person? It's always disconcerting to take a look inward, because it's usually not a pretty sight. Jesus declared that "what comes out of a man is what makes him 'unclean.' For from within, out of men's hearts, come evil thoughts, sexual immorality, theft, murder, adultery, greed, malice, deceit, lewdness, envy, slander, arrogance and folly. All these evils come from inside and make a man 'unclean' " (Mark 7:20-23). The timbre of my speech reveals what's being played out in my heart. I hate to admit the times I've snipped at someone because deep inside I was envious, angry, judgmental, or bitter. It all boils down to attitudes in my life that have to be confronted. Gossip often signals a deeper problem to be acknowledged, confessed, and forgiven.

What can I do to avoid being pulled into gossip? I've found that a little advance planning, as well as prayer, help prepare me for social or business situations that can easily turn into gossip fests. I try to mentally review polite conversational dodges I can make to avoid discussions that are taking a destructive turn. Recently a friend of mine was discussing her boss, and her comments started to drift into personal attacks. I casually diverted the conversation by shifting the topic to her upcoming vacation. But sometimes it's necessary to speak up and say, "Let's change the subject. I don't feel comfortable with what we're talking about."

From Today's Christian Woman
(January/February 1991)

Make It Happen

1. Rehearse in your mind what you said today. Did you say anything about another co-worker that you would not have said directly to her face? If so, ask the Lord for forgiveness and for his Spirit to help control your tendency to talk about others.

2. Study yourself and discover what conditions lead you to gossip. When you're feeling insecure about the project at work, do you tend to start talking about others? If you get bored, does your mouth go into overdrive? Learn to do something constructive when the tendency to talk is strong—write out your thoughts, read a short article, or call your husband.

3. Look up the following verses in the Bible about gossip: Galatians 5:15, 1 Corinthians 13:6, 1 Thessalonians 4:11, and James 4:11-12. Based on these verses, what do you think God has to say about the dangers and harm of gossip? Why do you think there are so many references throughout the Bible regarding how Christians use their words?

Chapter 5

HOW CAN I DRAW MY CO-WORKERS TO CHRIST?
Judith Briles

his morning I talked to a Denver-based group of salespeople called S.W.A.P. (Salesmen With A Purpose). It was a small group of twenty-five men and women. And as always at my speaking engagements, a table displays my books and tapes for sale at the conclusion.

Since the topic of my presentation was confidence, I brought several copies of the book *The Confidence Factor*, about ten copies of *When God Says No*, and a handful of copies of assorted other books I've written. When I packed up, several of my books remained, but every copy of *When God Says No* had been taken.

After the presentation, a man named Jerry stopped to chat. "I've been trying to analyze what happened this morning. We've had speakers before bring their merchandise and it's rare they sell anything. And on top of that, you really kept the group hooked this morning."

I thought about his comments for a few moments and then looked back on what had happened. I met a group of people I'd never met before, yet at the end of my speech I'd shared a little about my family, about my personal struggles, about my business, and how at each crossroad in my life faith was a factor.

While I wasn't overt in sharing my faith, it was indeed evident.

"What happened," I told Jerry, "is that I invited people in—I was real, I was open."

And that, I think, is one of the first steps in sharing Christ with our co-workers. Be real. Be true to who you are. In my case, that means being a Christian who is not afraid to show my own failings and compassion toward others.

In the short time during that breakfast meeting, I let others know that I'd been in their footsteps, that I could identify with

Simply Irresistable

If you want to introduce co-workers to Christ, you have to make him irresistible by the way you behave, by the things you say, by the way you treat people. These are the true measure of who you are. It's not how many widgets you can turn out in one day but rather how you treat others.

—Luci

how each person felt—I shared my compassion for them.

Closely related to compassion for our co-workers is the ability to listen—and I mean really listen—to those we work with daily. When we take the time to stop and listen to others with our hearts, a message comes through loud and clear—*I value you*. I have found again and again, when you let others know you value them, a kind of bonding occurs. For instance, the sales group I talked with this morning *knew* for a fact that I could relate to their frustrations. I came from a successful sales background in an era when few women were in sales. After the presentation, many came up to chat, to share their hurts. Although I would only know these people for a short time, I took time to listen. I was all ears, eyes, and heart.

As we move about the marketplace, I'm more and more convinced that we do ourselves a disservice when we're loud about our faith. We don't need to wear a badge that says, "I'm a Christian" or "Christ is my Savior." I spend a great deal of my time and energies in the secular market. If I plastered the wall of my office with posters that quote Scripture or used Christian jargon in every other sentence I spoke, people would label me a "Jesus freak." They'd say, "She's going to pester me—I'd better stay away." Overt labels can impede the process of winning others to Christ.

I'm confident a more subtle approach in the workplace is best. Many times after a presentation, I've had members of the audience come forward and say, "I knew you were a Christian. I could just tell." I have had women approach me after speaking and ask me to pray with them. So whatever I said opened a door!

Your beliefs are going to come through without shouting. If people comment on the fact that you seem at peace and focused—and I'm sure they will—share your reasons why. I often start with saying, "My peace comes because God is my partner."

What's equally important for Christians who work with nonbelievers is fitting in—in our dress, in our mannerisms, in our talk—as long as it doesn't compromise our principles. When our co-workers see someone who looks "normal" on the outside, they tend to be less threatened by our faith. They realize our faith isn't some cult, something that has swept us away and makes us alien to them. I think fitting in

A Single Light

A friend of mine worked at a very intense, dog-eat-dog pace—the office atmosphere was tremendously stressful. Everyone was edgy except one man. He worked as hard as the others, yet he was peaceful. Finally, she asked, "How can you stay calm when everyone else is crazy?"

"The only reason I can think of is I'm a Christian," he responded.

"But I am, too," she said.

"Do you read your Bible?" he asked.

"No," my friend admitted.

"Why don't you try it. Maybe it will help," he said, and then suggested she start with the Book of John.

Although my friend would go home at night dead tired, she made herself read and found she couldn't put her Bible down. She fell in love with Jesus and even led her husband to the Lord. Today they are totally on fire for the Lord. Yet all her co-worker did was be the light for one seeking soul. When he was asked a question he was ready to give an answer.

—Mary

with our co-workers in this sense does more for sharing our faith than all the labels we wear, all the Christian tapes we keep in our desk, or all the bits of Scripture we might recite.

Remember, as Christians we need to be real and approachable. And one of the first steps toward this end is to fit in with others socially.

Of course, we've all worked in situations at one time or another where a co-worker is cynical about the Christian faith. Quite possibly this co-worker crossed paths with an individual who gave Christianity a bad reputation. If this is the case, be sensitive to the fact that your co-workers may see your faith as judgmental, uncaring, and hypocritical.

But don't use this as an excuse to shy away from sharing Christ. Consider it your opportunity to undo the damage that has been done. We can break the preconceived notions of what a Christian looks like, sounds like, and acts like.

I know that I break some of the stereotypes by working mostly in secular markets. Not long ago, one of the men at the radio station where I do my show said, "I didn't know you'd written the book *When God Says No*. It's amazing what you learn about people." Such an insight helped this man realize that being a Christian in the marketplace doesn't mean you must confine yourself to strictly Christian markets.

Casting Out Lines

As others get to know you and you have a greater opportunity to share with them, consider what kind of words, or hooks, you can use to entice your co-workers to want to know more. Reciting Scripture verses at the drop of a hat doesn't do a lot for making you an approachable person. In fact, I've seen co-workers back off mentally—even physically—when they see this coming.

Instead, I rely strongly on Proverbs—a book that offers such universal messages. I'll often say, "I love the writing in Proverbs." Such an approach is rarely threatening. After all, the need for wisdom applies to everyone's life daily.

Words can also help you gauge how much and when to share your faith. For instance, when I'm doing a speech I throw in the fact that I've written a book about managing your money from a biblical perspective, called *Faith and Savvy, Too!* (Regal) and *Judith Brile's Money Guide for Christian Women* (Regal). How does the word "faith" register? I test the waters, and if the group seems receptive, I continue.

Remember, co-workers don't need to be beaten over the head with our faith. A lot of people say, "But there are times when you have to use your club." I agree those times exist. But more often than not, a gentler approach works best.

As you share your faith and the message of Jesus, look for clues to determine where a co-worker is spiritually. One of the women in the audience I spoke to this morning worked for a cosmetic company whose credo is to put God first, then family, then work. Immediately that puts you on common ground and offers you an opening to share.

Or consider the JCPenney Company, founded on the Golden Rule. Before I worked with this company, I did my research and found out about the company's background. I felt comfortable sharing my faith with them because I knew it's part of their heritage, too.

While we can do a little "research" on our co-workers, it won't always be that evident where they are spiritually. So I challenge you to keep your eyes and ears open as you get to know your co-workers. You never know where the Lord might leave a door open.

I remember one person saying to me, "You know, the Jewish and Christian faiths are really very similar."

"How so?" I asked, and the person went through a litany of similarities.

And then I said, "There is one central belief, one biggie that you overlooked that belongs at the top. Christians believe Jesus was the Son of God, while Jews believe he was a great man, a great teacher. To me this is a very significant difference."

Our discussion didn't go much further, but I'm certain the words we exchanged kept that man thinking. While we might not touch all of our co-workers or see them accept Christ, we can at least leave them thinking. And sometimes that's not a bad way to go.

Walking Your Talk

One of my favorite sayings is "walk your talk." Check yourself from time to time. Are you true to what you're saying, by how you're behaving? Do you really care for others? Are you free from malice and spite? Have you chosen not to gossip? When you see someone hurting, do you say, "What can I do to help?" Have you taken the time to develop your listening skills so you come across as a willing listener who is able to tune in quickly? If you're not the right person to be listening to your co-worker's needs, have you taken the time to steer her to someone who is better equipped to help?

We all know what a bitter impression hypocrites leave. No matter how noble the cause, if their walk doesn't match their talk, they lose credibility. Take Arnold Schwarzenegger, the actor who is serving as chairman of the President's Council on Physical Fitness and Sports and promoting the education and health of children. That is indeed a worthwhile cause. Yet, I personally find it hard to reconcile his positive message with the fact that he gets millions of dollars for producing and starring in films that perpetuate violence.

Confidence in sharing our Christian "walk and talk" comes in part with age. Experience refines our talk and, I believe, makes it easier for us to walk it. At times we wish we could come to the marketplace with an exciting, perfect, and wonderful background to share with our co-workers. But few of us have such a background, and besides, that's not what draws our co-workers to us and to Christ.

As Christians we can share the Lord and how he gives us the direction and strength to move beyond painful experiences in our life. God uses us as we are, in the job where he has placed us, to share with others the hope we have in Christ.

Make It Happen

1. Realize you don't have to be perfect to share Christ. This thinking can paralyze us from moving forward. Be open and honest with your co-workers about the triumphs and trials you've experienced and how the Lord has helped you. Consider keeping a spiritual journal that shows when prayer was answered or God was at work in your life. Then when others ask about your faith, you can share more easily that God is active and present in your life.

2. Rate your listening skills. Here are some skills good listeners use: They focus on what the speaker is saying and don't think up a reply while she is talking. They look for the feelings behind the words. They ask questions that draw a person out—questions that are generated by compassion not curiosity. Good listeners reflect back what they hear.

Remember, you can learn to be a better listener if you make a dedicated effort. Don't use the excuse that your personality doesn't make you a good listener.

3. Read your Bible. Without a firm foundation in the Scriptures, it's nearly impossible to share your faith. If you're not currently involved in a Bible study, consider joining one. Keep your Christian fellowship active—it's a valuable resource as you go out into the world to share Christ.

Who, Me? Give a Testimony?

Debra Petrosky

What powerful tool does the most mild-mannered Christian woman have that even skeptics, atheists, and New Agers can't refute? Her testimony! Many women feel intimidated about sharing their faith when they're toe to toe with an intellectual or the local cultist who arrives on their doorstep. But with a little practice and forethought, your testimony can make others thirsty for the gospel.

The following hints will help you confidently tell what God has done in your life. When evaluating your testimony, ask these questions:

Is it fresh? Think about where you would be today if Christ hadn't transformed your life. How has God intervened in your life in tangible, specific ways? A testimony of God's provision makes a great lead-in.

Is it focused? Have you eliminated the trivia? Your listener probably doesn't need to know that you got saved on a snowy, windswept night in December. Outline your testimony using these three steps:

a. What my life was like before Christ
b. How I came to know him
c. What my life is like now

Focus on one facet of your life and how it has changed. Contrast the guilt you carried with the forgiveness you now enjoy in Christ. Explain how a new sense of purpose replaced your former aimlessness. Instead of reminiscing about the pleasures of sin, give equal time to your life since conversion.

If you came to Christ as a child, it may be more appropriate to focus on ways God has helped you through certain situations, or how he has demonstrated faithfulness, love, and guidance in specific, concrete ways.

Eliminate any "Christianese" that might confuse an unbeliever. You may know what it means to be "washed in the blood," but such phraseology generates raised eyebrows—not interest.

Is it flexible? You may not have an hour to tell your entire story to the gas attendant who fills your tank. Do you have a shorter version for those occasions? You may have only enough time to say, "Sir, since yielding my life to Jesus Christ, I've never enjoyed life more. Here's a tract for you to read in your spare time (or during your break)."

Be able to relate your testimony in three to five minutes. Write it out on a sheet of paper and ask your husband or friend to critique it. The apostle Paul exhorts us to be "fitted with the readiness that comes from the gospel of peace" (Ephesians 6:15). Take time to get prepared.

People may not fall at your feet and ask to be saved after hearing your testimony, but they should leave considering eternal issues. Your personal account of God's faithfulness can draw them one step closer to the Cross.

From Today's Christian Woman
(March/April 1990)

LIFE ON A TIGHTROPE

opple, a popular children's game, could easily be renamed *The Working Woman*. The game's concept is simple—a plate with a small indentation at the center rests on a pedestal. Multi-colored discs are stacked on the plate until one piece, placed on the precariously balanced plate, brings the tower crashing down.

The parallel between a working woman's balancing act and the game is undeniable. The only difference? In the game everyone laughs when the plate falls off its pedestal. For the working woman, role upon role upon role builds frustration and intensifies the pressures of everyday life.

Just how can we balance our lives when the blocks on our plate only get higher and higher? Is a cookbook of twenty-nine-minute meals the answer? Another to-do list? A monthly organizer? A personal secretary? Hardly. The answer, as Judith, Mary, and Luci explain, is to better know yourself—your own strengths and weaknesses, gifts and abilities—and to better know God and listen to him daily.

Chapter 6

HOW CAN I BALANCE MY MANY PRIORITIES?
Judith Briles

chieving a balance between the demands of a job and the many other responsibilities we juggle is seldom easy. One responsibility may dominate the picture for a while, only to be edged out by another, more pressing priority. Women seem particularly adept at pursuing too many opportunities at once, only to make sacrifices in every area just to keep all the balls in the air. At the same time, we seem equally prone to second-guessing ourselves—to wondering if we've made the best choices.

While I'm thankful women are finally admitting superwoman doesn't exist, the reality is we're forced to live out dual roles. So how do we go about making decisions and sacrifices to achieve some type of balance between our personal lives and our jobs?

An excellent way to start is with a simple exercise I use at many of my seminars. Stop reading for a moment and think about what activities are most important to you and what ones are not. Now take a piece of paper and tear it into quarters. Write down one of your top four priorities on each section. It could be starting a family, switching jobs, committing yourself to a Bible

study, confronting a co-worker, or developing a budding friend‑
ship—whatever is most important to *you*.

Hold these four choices in your hand. Look them over and
pick the one that ranks lowest in priority. Crumple it up and toss
it away. Now, of the three papers left, pick the one that is least
important and throw it away. Of the two papers left, decide which
is less important. Throw it away. Now look at the piece of paper
you have left.

Is this truly your top priori‑
ty? Is this what you're concen‑
trating on? Is this what you're
doing to be true to who you are
and what your main goal in life
is? Surprisingly, as you look at
that remaining paper, the answer
might be no.

If this is the case, it's time
to prioritize. The only way to achieve a sense of balance in your
life is to know who you are—what is truly important to you and
what isn't. Once you begin to sort out your true priorities, you
can make choices that will lead you in the direction you want to
go. The exercise you just did is a start. But knowing yourself is a
process. To continue discovering where your gifts and ambitions
lie, it's imperative that you begin listening to your inner voice.

We all have one, whether it comes from our head, our
heart, or our gut. The problem is, most of us ignore it. What I do
to tune in to my inner voice is ask myself a series of questions
every night when I go to bed. "Okay, God, what did we do
today? What do we need to plan for tomorrow? Where are we?
What worked? What didn't work?" On a daily basis, I take time
to assess my life—to really listen to what God is saying to me.

Listening to yourself is key to having confidence in the

Time You Can Count On

*You have to carve out time in your
day for the Lord—it has to be your
highest priority. If you don't carve it
out, it won't happen. Although I have
a great deal of time to call my own, I
still have to set aside time with God and
not let anything take its place. I've
found I must have that time in order to
make good choices, to hear his voice,
and stay in control. When I get away
from my daily time with the Lord I go
downhill spiritually, mentally, and
emotionally.*

—Mary

decisions you make each day and throughout your life. It provides you with a snapshot of yourself that you can pull up and know what fits and what doesn't fit the picture.

Put It on Paper

I've worked in the business world for years, and if there's one common thread that runs through companies, it's that most have a mission statement. This document, usually concise, answers simple questions like "What is our business?" or "What do we hope our business can become?" It offers a sense of direction—something that guides a company as it makes decisions and sets priorities.

Be True to You

For years I tried to be like my brother Chuck, because I so admired his success. To my surprise, I later learned there was a period of time he had tried to be like me. What I realized is that it's important to get to know yourself— to value your unique gifts. You need to develop your own style that is true to you. The people we admire the most are uniquely themselves.

—Luci

I currently serve on the Miss America Advisory Council. One of our objectives was to bring a voice to Miss America; that is, establish a clear purpose for her, linking her platform with today's concerns. Without a doubt, she's an attractive, intelligent, and talented woman. But she could accomplish more if she had a mission statement—a focus. So we've been working at developing one for each new Miss America. Debbye Turner's (1990) platform was striving for excellence in the inner city, Majory Vincent's (1991) was drawing attention to domestic violence, and Carolyn Sapp's (1992) platform focused on involving everyone in improving education.

I think every woman owes it to herself to write her own mission statement. While it may not focus on social concerns as ours have for Miss America, it will create a structure for you to work from. Ask yourself some simple questions like, "Who am I?" "What are my gifts and talents?" "How can I best use them?" "What do I hope for in life?"

One part of my personal mission statement is to help women empower other women. I think we need to honor, support, and encourage one another—especially in the work world. Because I see this as part of my calling in life, I have made choices that fulfill this area of my mission statement. My speaking and writing have consistently been directed at women. Whether it's about money, confidence, leadership—my intended audience is always women. God has blessed me with communication skills, and I feel I would be violating the gifts he has entrusted me with if I didn't share them with other women.

When you write a mission statement for yourself, you'll be surprised at how it can renew your focus as well as help you set priorities. On New Year's Day, or at another set time during the year, write yourself a letter that describes your mission. Once you have this on paper, work up some goals that are in line with it. Suddenly, enrolling in a company-sponsored MBA program may be out of sync with what you've found as your true mission—to start a business at home.

Beating the Guilt Rap

Even when we have a clear sense of what we want to do with our lives, working women in particular still try to do it all. Almost guaranteed, we fail. And then guilt creeps in, sabotaging our best efforts to meet our goals and maintain a balanced life.

Sometimes what moves us beyond guilt is a crisis. The breakthrough for me—when I finally realized I couldn't do it all—was the death of my infant son. Until then, I always said, "I have to do this. I have to do that." When Billy died, I learned to stop. Though I had two grade-school children and a preschooler at the time Billy died, I needed to take time to heal. I listened to music, I painted, I lived the serenity prayer. I could not change Billy dying, but I could change how I spent my time. I consciously decided that my house was not going to be perfect—not a pig sty, but not immaculate either. So what if I didn't vacuum every other day. The dust would always be there tomorrow. My children might not.

But why wait for a crisis like I did to shake up your life and make you assess your priorities? Sometimes a quick reality check is all it takes to get you back on track if you're wrestling with guilt or feeling unsure about decisions you've made. When this happens to me I reach for a piece of paper and complete these two statements: "I'm feeling guilty about . . . " and "I'm feeling guilty because . . . "

What is making you feel uneasy or guilty? Is it a spouse? A parent? Your kids? Yourself? Is the feedback from your friends or church contributing to your guilt feelings?

The other way to determine whether you're feeling legitimate or false guilt is to call on a friend who listens, someone who is caring and supportive of you and your goals in life and who is nonjudgmental. She will act as a sounding board as you sort out your feelings.

Lending an Ear

As a working woman it's important to remember that you may have a multitude of listeners because different women will understand different portions of your life. Let's say a situation at work has thrown your life out of balance. Try finding a friend at work who understands the challenges you face at the office, someone who knows your work conditions. However, a word of caution is important—be discerning in whom you trust with your vulnerabilities.

Say you come to work one morning, completely preoccupied with thoughts of your teenage daughter. At break time, you casually say to a co-worker, "I don't know what to do with my daughter. I'm not sure how I'll survive these teen years." An innocent remark echoed by millions of parents of teens worldwide.

The person you happened to share your frustration with appeared to be a caring listener. Yet, soon after this incident, there's a promotion opportunity. You're qualified, so is your co-worker. She gets the job, you don't. A peek at your personnel file uncovers a notation by management showing concerns about giving you added responsibility because of your home situation. Outrageous—and it happens every day.

So it's important to recognize that if we share our concerns, fears, and sometimes dreams, with someone who is not really our advocate, it could create added problems.

As you choose listeners in your life, it also pays to seek out positive people. A negative co-worker can easily fuel your insecurities, your fears, and your guilt. And as you absorb your co-worker's negativism, soon your energy also will be depleted.

Our daily lives are full of variables, so it's important to realize that who we invite into our lives—those we work with and those who are our friends—will impact how we feel about the decisions and sacrifices we make as working women. The "self-talk" we all engage in greatly affects our outlook too.

Former first lady Eleanor Roosevelt's words have been one of my guideposts: "No one can make you feel inferior without your permission." Wise words loaded with common sense. Add them to your toolbox.

When you try something new ask yourself, How does this feel? Do I like it? Is it uncomfortable? If so, why? Because I've never done it before? Because my mother said I shouldn't?

The voice of your upbringing may say you can't do something but you have to bring in an empowering voice—God's—that says, "Yes, you can, but you must listen to how I'm directing you."

Even the woman who is in tune with God's lead will struggle to maintain a balanced life. There are going to be times when each of us is out of step at work or in our personal lives. Just being open and receptive to the fact that life is not going to be perfect helps bring perspective back into a busy working woman's life. God may not provide us with a perfectly ordered life, but what he does provide is himself, his presence, and open doors that bring us closer to being productive, positive, and realistic working Christian women.

Time to Trim
Judith Couchman

You really wanted to teach that Sunday school class. And it seemed only natural to plan monthly social activities for your family. But then you added symphony guild, tutoring at the YWCA, taking a management course . . . . Worthwhile activities? Yes. But they'll render you worthless if you overextend yourself. Here's how to tell when it's time to trim your schedule:

1. *Feeling out of control.* Who's running your life? You or your schedule? When your to-do list is about to do you in, when there's a gnawing feeling that at any moment you'll spin out of control, it's time to slow down. Involvement doesn't mean letting a schedule push you around.

2. *Eating and running.* If you've memorized the menu at a local fast-food restaurant, it's not a good sign. Eating on the run doesn't promote smooth digestion, family togetherness, or overall well being. This week count the times you eat on the run. More than twice? You're short-changing your health and your relationships (and probably gaining weight).

3. *Forgetting God.* Doesn't this sound familiar? "Lord, I did it again. I didn't spend time with you. I'll try to do better tomorrow." If you're ending the day with apologies instead of prayers, your priorities need an overhaul. Regular time with God strengthens you for each day's tasks.

4. *Squelching social time.* Your husband surprises you with theater tickets for tonight. Your friend asks you

to go shopping Saturday morning. The kids want you to attend a movie with them. How do you respond? Too tired? Too much to do? When you're saying "no" too often, involvements may be turning you into a drone. All work and no play makes Jill a very dull woman—with a dwindling list of friends.

5. *Raging emotions.* Do little mishaps disturb you? Are you angry and don't know why? Do you cry easily? An overextended schedule could be making you uptight. Cutting back activities, sleeping more and allowing for leisure may put you back on track.

6. *Ongoing physical problems.* Headaches, skin rashes, twitching eyes, upset stomachs, irregularity, or chronic fatigue could indicate you're on stress overload. If you keep barreling ahead, bigger physical problems may surface. Along with a physical checkup, slowing down could be the best remedy.

7. *Missing the joy.* Do you dread attending meetings? Is helping out a hassle? Are you counting the weeks until it's all over? When the joy of giving drains from your involvements, when you'd rather be anywhere else, it's probably best to evaluate your commitments.

8. *Increasing conflicts.* Is your family frustrated that you're never home? Are you crabby with friends? Does your life feel caught in the crossfire? Harmonious relationships don't just happen. They need the nurture of a balanced lifestyle.

From Today's Christian Woman
(September/October 1989)

Make It Happen

1. Look for a woman you admire for her ability to keep a balanced perspective while fulfilling several different roles. Invite her to lunch, meet for coffee, or set up a phone-chat appointment and informally ask her how she manages and what she has learned along the way.

2. Think back over the messages you received during your upbringing. Using constructive self-talk, work on erasing those tapes in your mind that say you *should* do certain things, like cooking a four-course meal every night when in reality that doesn't fit with your life. Wipe the slate clean and bring to it new ideas and solutions that work for your unique situation.

3. Make a list of all activities you're involved in. Carefully study the list. Do you *really* want to be involved in each activity? Have you spread yourself too thin? Are other areas of your life suffering? Prayerfully consider cutting back the list.

4. Make it a practice when you are asked to add responsibilities either at home or in the office, to think it through first. Have a standard response, such as, "I'd like to think about that. Could I get back to you tomorrow?" Then go home and review your commitments. Will this new request topple the cart or can you honestly handle it? Saying no is nothing to be ashamed of if you're listening to yourself and God.

Chapter 7

HOW MUCH OF MY IDENTITY SHOULD I DERIVE FROM MY WORK?
Luci Swindoll

e all have the potential to lose our identity in almost anything we do. It can happen at home. It can happen in a marriage. And it can certainly happen in the workplace. Suddenly you wonder, "Who am I?"

The first step in determining how much of our identity we should derive from our work begins with asking a simple question: Exactly what is identity? To me, identity is what makes me who I am as an individual. It's the distinguishing personality of Luci Swindoll, and it is inseparable from anything I do—whether I'm Christian Luci, businesswoman Luci, or friend Luci. So ask yourself, What is it that makes me an individual? What is it about me that is like no one else?

Once you have a handle on these questions, then you can ask yourself some specific questions about your work, such as, How would I classify my work? Is it *just* a job? My profession? Or my calling?

A job is something we may not want to do, but it serves a purpose—like helping pay the bills or putting food on the table. A profession, on the other hand, requires something more—an education. To pursue a profession, say medicine or singing opera,

75

you must have additional training beyond high school.

However, a calling is something inescapable, almost inbred. The artist Michelangelo, for example, couldn't do anything but sculpt and paint. He was driven by it with a passion. That was his calling.

A Rock-Solid Identity

One of the most important attributes of God is his steadfast nature. Have you ever considered what it would be like to go to bed at night and wonder if God would be the same tomorrow? To not know what he would be like from day to day? Because of his dependable nature we can put our confidence and trust in him.

—Mary

The closer our work is to our calling, the more likely we are to merge our identity with what we do for a living. I look at my brother Chuck, who is pastor of the First Evangelical Free Church in Fullerton, California. He's never wanted to do anything but preach. Even as a child he was memorizing poetry and learning Scripture. He practiced his speaking skills on the whole family. He was very involved in drama and speech in high school. As a result, all his life he has pursued his calling to preach. His work, therefore, is not merely a job where he puts in eight hours a day. It's his passion! His work fulfills his calling.

I'll admit there is a lot of me that would like my identity to come from my job. After all, we spend so many hours at the workplace, I think it would be gratifying to have a job that fulfills, at least in part, who we are as individuals. But by the same token, I wouldn't want to be known only for my work. All my life I've wanted a career, and I've loved my career, but I've always wanted other things as well. I don't want to be known just for being good in my chosen profession. I want a balanced life. Even if my work was my calling, I would want to have time for friends and other interests.

It isn't wrong to seek a certain amount of your identity from your job, especially if your work is in line with your calling. However, those who can say their work is their calling are a fortunate few. Life isn't usually that tidy. The rest of us must work at keeping a sense of balance between who we are and what we do.

Memories of Me

As we struggle with determining if our work is a good fit with our overall identity, it helps to ask yourself, How do I want to be remembered? Do I want people to remember me for what I do or for who I am? Personally, I want to be remembered for who I am. But again, there's the rub: who I am is very much tied up in what I do.

Here's a quick litmus test to see where you find your identity.

The Family Factor
Even today, having held jobs from stockbroker to financial consultant to public speaker, I clearly believe one of my most important roles is being a mother. Of course, that role has changed over the years. Now I'm a grandmother, but its importance hasn't diminished. I'm encouraged to see more men and women realize the significance of family as they define their careers and what is of lasting value.
—Judith

If you are introduced to someone, note how long it takes before you identify yourself with your work. If defining yourself means giving out your job title, then it's time to stop and think. If your work identity permeates every single thing you do, you probably need to seek some balance in your life.

I've noticed in Europe that people are hesitant to ask about occupation. They're not the least bit hesitant to ask how much you paid for the blouse you're wearing, but what you do is considered private. And yet if you're in a conversation with an American it's not too long before you're asked, "Well, what do you do?"

Society demands that I find a label for myself. Yet the most interesting people I know are those who are genuinely themselves and don't attempt to tie their identity to their work. These people are without pretense, and while there aren't many like them, they are refreshing. I have one friend in particular who is an interior decorator, college graduate, mother, grandmother, and traveler. She's happy in each role, and I can't remember a time when any one of them was more dominant than the other.

I enjoy her so much as a *person*. Her many-faceted personality makes her comfortable to be with and permits me to be who I am without labels attached.

In addition, people like this let you be you. They don't try to straighten you out and make you into something you are not.

Getting to the Source

As Christians, we know that our basic identity is in Christ. But I don't think we stop often enough to consider what this really means. We are more inclined to dwell on what we do and who we are—the urgent and the superficial. Our identity in Christ is once and for all established when we put our faith in him. And yet, many of us don't consciously dwell on this profound reality. We simply go about *living* our lives rather than *thinking* about their significance in Christ—thus blinding us from knowing who we truly are.

We can develop our sense of security and identity in Christ as we spend time with him in prayer, offer our conscious praise to him, and give him the credit for all we are and have. The more of his Word we put into our lives, the more aware we become that he is our prime motivator. When we simply take him at his word, we find he is utterly trustworthy. This also creates opportunity for his Spirit to be manifested in our lives and work.

When the Bottom Drops Out

As Christians, our self-esteem lies in loving ourselves because Christ loves us. In his eyes we are acceptable however or whoever we are. Whether we admit it or not, though, our self-esteem often rests largely on our work. Many of us don't realize the extent to which we base our identity on our work until that work is taken from us. If you've ever been fired, laid off, or have quit a job for other reasons, the connection between your work and self-esteem becomes all too clear. In situations like these, it's not uncommon for self-esteem to plunge. If this happens, I would advise you to do two things.

First, seek out spiritual guidance from a friend you can trust, who can keep a confidence, and who is also growing spiritually. With this friend's help, you can sift through your pain and the emotions—good and bad—that accompany loss of a job. And you can learn to better understand yourself. Proverbs 20:5 says, "Counsel in the heart of man is like deep water. But a man of understanding will draw it out" (NKJV). In other words, counsel can be found within ourselves, but it needs to be "drawn out" by a friend's understanding.

Second, find time to be alone. I put a lot of stock in solitude. I've lived alone for more than twenty years. And though I have a lot of friends, there are times when I still need to get away and regroup. While I might experience a modicum of loneliness, in the end I'm richer for the solitude. From my own experience, I know that everyone can benefit from quiet time, especially if you're sorting through a work-related crisis as it effects your self-image.

Besides the possible damage to our self-esteem that can occur when our identity comes solely from our work, there is another important reason to separate who we are from what we do. When we tie who we are too closely with our work, we end up being harder on ourselves than necessary. Let me explain what I mean.

Let's say I've had a really bad day at work. I messed up an important project, and I know others must be thinking that I'm the biggest goof-up they've ever worked with. My day may be a loss, but if my identity isn't based only on my job, I'm then better able to keep mistakes in perspective.

Are you going to wallow in your troubles and risk being sidelined forever? Or will you get your motor running and confess, "I goofed. Tomorrow's another day. I'm going to try again." With experience, you'll learn like I did that a single mistake seldom tarnishes your reputation. And experience helps us to quit making the same old mistakes over and over.

Moreover, when I have a bad day, it only proves to me I'm human. The Lord has said he will be our strength in our weakness. There was a time when I might have died over a blunder at work. But now I know life goes on. In Romans 8:1, Paul says there is no condemnation in Christ. We, in our humanity, may fail, but we are not failures.

Red Flags to Watch For

Without a doubt, you can get in a work situation that is really exciting and wonderful. And almost without your knowing it, your identity can become tied up in what you do. How can you tell when you're leaning too heavily on your work for a sense of identity?

Four types of behavior stand out as red flags. The first is feeling the need to toot your own horn. If you're good at what you do, people will know it. You don't have to go around saying, "This is a piece of cake. I'll have no problem here because I'm good at what I do." Your work will speak for itself.

Hoping to win by intimidating is another red flag. When I worked at Mobil Oil, a co-worker once said to me, "Luci, you'll never be a good leader unless you have the power of intimidation." I said, "I don't want to intimidate. To me intimidation is stress producing. Instead, I want respect—respect that is genuinely earned." I've always thought that if I'm a Christian and I handle myself as a woman of God and as a professional, without being prudish, people will respect that and respect me.

The third red flag is taking credit where credit *isn't* due. For example, the ideas or the finished product was a team effort, yet you lead others to believe it was your work alone. When an individual's self-confidence is shaky this often happens—especially if the job is well done.

The final red flag to watch out for is becoming overly concerned about your image at work. If that's the case, it may be time to take stock of where your self-esteem comes from. If you find yourself wringing your hands over every decision you make at work—good or bad—you need to do a reality check. Ask yourself, Is the outcome of this decision truly that vital?

———

My relationship with Christ is, in my words, my proto-plasm—the living matter that makes life possible and permeates everything I do. Wherever I go, Christ is in me, and I am in him. He's my identifying foundation. It's with this assurance—this sense of identity—that I am able to keep going when I've had a bad day at work or my career isn't all I've hoped. These daily trials and troubles are only of temporary importance. What is eternal is who I am in Christ. And once I've got that firmly established, the other factors that play into my overall identity—like work—fall into place.

Make It Happen

1. If you don't consider your work to be your calling, or your job is not as satisfying as you'd like it to be, look at your life overall for balance. Are your friendships growing and rewarding? Have you added any new interests to your life in the past year? Are you finding ways to use your talents that are honoring to the Lord? Remember, balance is the key.

2. For a moment, pretend you don't have a career. Now describe yourself. What makes you a unique creation of God? How do you feel when your work is not a part of your description? Are you at a loss? In your own words, what does it mean to be Christ-centered?

3. Decide if your work is a job, a profession, or a calling. If it currently isn't your calling, then consider reading up on understanding your gifts and talents. Pray that God might help you uncover your calling and lead you to ways that your gifts can be used to glorify him.

4. Consider having a close and trusted friend describe who you are. Do you agree? Be open to your friend's perspective. You may be surprised—she might see something you've completely overlooked.

Chapter 8

HOW DO I MAKE
TIME FOR ME?
Luci Swindoll

t seemed like each time my friend and I were together she talked about work: "All I do is work. Yes, it's exciting, fun, fulfilling. But it's all I do. And it doesn't seem right."

In her midforties, my friend is energetic, bright, interesting, well-traveled, and competent. But I too shared her concern about her time-consuming work habits. Even though her work was in "ministry," her schedule was much like that of a workaholic in the secular world.

I began to encourage her to venture into other areas, to broaden her experience and her life. I planned trips for us, outings to museums and plays. I suggested she incorporate more fun into her life, more time for play. I asked questions which forced her into realms of conversation she was unaccustomed to exploring. Slowly but surely, she began to relax and look forward to times set aside for sheer pleasure.

She broke out of those thought patterns she had reinforced with steel. She stopped being a slave to thinking all of life must revolve around doing something strategic or that unless she was accomplishing something "important" every minute, life was being wasted. In short, she became a human *being* instead of a human *doing*.

After a time, my friend freed herself from the bondage of a workaholic lifestyle. She will always love her work. But she's stopped worrying about it so much. She says she's learned that God has not only a task for each of us to accomplish but a life to live as well. He wants to fill our lives so they will be whole, balanced, and full of his joy.

Personal time for yourself is essential to round out who you are. It's vital. Without it you end up giving everything you are to everyone else and there's no time or energy left for you to enjoy life.

To be perfectly honest, finding time to do those things I like and enjoy hasn't been a tremendous struggle for me because I've always loved to have a good time. I've always created personal time to pursue my own interests. To play. In my thirty-year career with Mobil Oil, I did many things in my spare time. I sang in the opera, I did art projects, I wrote books, I spoke at various meetings, I traveled, I even studied another language. I never was content just being one thing.

Because solitude and the development of a personal life have been a priority despite a packed schedule, I've learned several ways to make time for myself.

I Flunked an Interview

When my children were young, I hired help with the housework for a few hours a week. It gave me time for activities that brought balance—playing with the kids, reading a book, taking a walk. Those few relaxing hours made me more productive at home and on the job. Soon after, a major woman's magazine wanted to interview me as one of the rising women in California. They asked, "How do you do it all?" My reply: "I get help." They didn't want to hear that. Instead, they wanted me to say on weekends I bake a week's worth of casseroles and freeze them. The editor literally said, "We can't tell our readers you get help." I responded, "Why not? Do your readers a favor and tell them it's okay to get some help."

—Judith

Passing the Buck

If you're going to work, you've got to learn to delegate. You simply cannot do everything yourself. Sure, I know people who want to do it all, and the idea of delegating is very difficult for them. But, if they don't delegate, they never have time for anything but work. Their in-basket is always full.

One woman I worked with at Mobil Oil stands out as an example of what can happen if you don't delegate. This woman wanted desperately to climb the corporate ladder. Eventually she got to the point where she would come early, spend the night in the ladies' room, get dressed there in the morning, and be at her desk before sunrise. She would do this three or four days at a time, thinking all along it was putting

Fresh Air

While it has not been easy, I'm trying to work exercise into my routine by walking each morning. It's such a great time for my mind to be open to God for ideas—to see possibilities I never saw before. Almost every time I walk, an insight comes into my head and I know I wouldn't have thought about it if I hadn't given myself time to mediate and be with the Lord.

—Mary

her ahead. But in reality it was putting her far behind. She looked like a zombie and felt awful, and besides, she grew crabbier each day. Finally she was fired because of her slovenly work. Her philosophy of working hard now to get ahead later backfired.

When you're trying to decide what to delegate, ask yourself "What can *and* can't I do well?" Realizing where your weaknesses are will give you some sense for what can be farmed out to others. For example, I can't style my hair well, so once (and sometimes twice) a week I go to the salon and get it professionally done. I look forward to this little pleasure and my mind is relieved because I don't have to fool with it. Look for those little time thieves that cause you distress. When you find others to help, you can end up with more prime time for yourself.

If You Can't Delegate, Relegate

Delegating isn't always possible though. Suppose I have a book deadline fast approaching. Obviously only I can write the book; I can't delegate the task. Or suppose I've been invited to speak at a meeting. I'm expected in person; I can't send a substitute. But to reduce the stress I feel from other pressures in my life, I can relegate, that is, establish lower priorities for my other interests.

Taking an art class, for example, will have to be a lower priority, or having company over for dinner will have to wait until I finish writing the book or fulfilling my speaking obligation. It boils down to doing things in the order of their importance. If you can get that simple truth wired into your thinking, you'll start to find more time for yourself.

Ask Away

Asking questions can also be an effective means of opening up more time. Pride often stops us from doing this and we stubbornly insist, I'm not going to ask anybody how to do this, that, or the other thing. Ultimately we end up spinning our wheels.

When I was offered a position as an executive at Mobil, I was afraid I wouldn't do a good job. I was the first woman to hold such a major management position in that division of Mobil and my self-esteem was a bit shaky. I phoned a friend in Dallas and admitted my fears to her. She said, "Luci, you're the perfect person for the job. Just remember: Don't be afraid to ask questions."

So when necessary, I began to ask questions of those higher up, those under me, and those who reported to me.

I saved myself time by asking "How do you do this," rather than doing it myself, finding out it wasn't right, and then doing it again. You won't look foolish asking questions. In fact, you'll probably look smart because you won't be wasting your time.

And it helps those around you because everybody wants to be asked questions. I remember the first time at Mobil someone asked me a question. I thought, I've arrived. They want to know *from me*.

Say Goodbye to Perfection

It's also possible to work something to death, and that can rob you of time. Learn to discern when you have spent enough money, time, and/or energy on a project. Study what you're doing and decide when enough is enough. For instance, I could write and rewrite and rewrite the chapter of a book until it became grains of sand. And in the long run, who cares? Instead I should try to say what I have to say the best I can and leave it at that. Sure, I may leave something out, but that's life. Do the best you can, then move on.

Making the Most of Time Alone

When our lives are jampacked with tasks and activities, the one thing that inevitably gets edged out is time alone. We tend to view thinking time as nonproductive time. Yet how much mental energy we would save if we just used our heads. During daily "quiet times" we can rehearse the day—thinking through possible options and choosing the best path. We'll then be less likely to make snap decisions that more often than not are the wrong decisions.

Remember your first date with someone you liked but didn't know too well. From friends, you found out a little about your date and then constructed some ideas of what you might talk about. In a sense, you've done your homework, you've prepared ahead. In the same way, you can use quiet time productively to decide what situations might arise to throw you off course during your work day. How will you compensate for the change in schedule? Thinking ahead can help alleviate a lot of the frustration that comes with trying to accomplish many things in a structured time frame.

As you use quiet time to reflect on the best use of your time and talents, you may also want to consider what rewards you are willing to defer. Everything cannot be done all at once.

Let's say you have a career path mapped out that involves additional education. For a while you may be out of the work force, or earning only a part-time salary. Yes, you'll have to forgo your normal salary, but in doing so your education will ultimately result in a higher salary. This goal gives you the impetus to defer present rewards.

Do You Have a Hobby?

As you attempt to find some personal time, don't underestimate the value of hobbies and projects. When I take time to read, visit a museum, or pursue a hobby, it makes me a more interesting person to be with. I have something to share with others that isn't work related.

I've always got something going—a stack of books I want to read, things I want to make with my hands, music I want to hear, paintings or sculpture I want to know more about, classes to take. For example, I find going to the symphony very quieting to my soul. It rejuvenates and enriches me.

I've also noticed when you have an interest or a hobby you're more reflective about how you use your personal time. Instead of aimlessly running off to the mall when you have a free moment, you're more likely to use the time productively.

For instance, several years ago I decided I would read six classics a year. I figured six was a reasonable number—that's one every two months. I started with *Alice in Wonderland*, a book I'd always wanted to read. As a result of this commitment, I had the most wonderful year reading six fabulous books I had never made time to read.

If you set your mind to it, you'll be amazed at how many extra activities you can add to your days. And over time, you'll feel the joy that comes from truly enjoying life. You'll be a richer person.

———◦◦◦———

Many Christian women are programmed to think, You must always give, always be selfless, always think of others. In

Scripture we're commanded to lay down our lives. That's a wonderful teaching, and I strongly adhere to its premise. But what do we really have to lay down if we haven't truly been living life? If we truly haven't been developing our identity, our individuality?

My brother has this saying: "Know yourself, like yourself, and be yourself." Don't be afraid to have a good time, to do those things you enjoy that fulfill you. It's completely biblical to value yourself—after all, you are a creation of God.

A good friend of mine put it this way. She says, "Everything I've ever done, I've never had time to do." Isn't that a great line? We tend to think, I have to do this, but I don't have time for that. Yet somehow, if it's a priority for us, we find time. We think, I'd like to fix a nice meal, but I don't have time. If we push ahead and do it, in the end we have a memory, a reflection, and a sense of joy from that accomplishment.

We can all look at the past, see unfulfilled dreams and hopes, and then chide ourselves. Or we can look to the future and think, Tomorrow is the day I need to plan for. Tomorrow I'll invite friends over when the house looks better and I have more money for a nicer meal. But beware: tomorrow is yesterday's today. It is the present. And a real key to creating personal time for myself is learning to live in this present day.

I'd like to see more women think, I have only ten dollars but I want to have three or four people over for dinner. I'll serve hamburgers. Not much—but it's a start. You will have a fun memory of that time, and soon you'll want to do it again. As you continue to enjoy your time and resources, you will richly add to the fabric of your life—one day at a time, making many threads that weave a beautiful tapestry.

If you live in the past, you'll be afraid to move forward. If you live in the future, you'll miss the beauty of today. Learn to love today.

That which we value we invest in. If we value our health, we get check-ups, eat right, and exercise. If we value friendships, we find time to have lunch together, share mutual hobbies, discuss family news, our joys and heartaches, or visit one another as often as possible. Likewise, if we value ourselves, we must find time to invest in our own development.

The truth is we really do reap what we sow. If I want to reap happiness, I've got to sow happiness. If I want to reap contentment, I must sow contentment. It's important to realize that we are worth investing in.

Anything of value will cost—be it time, energy, or money. Decide today what you're willing to pay for it. Are you willing to hire some help with the kids so you can take that class you've had your eye on for months? Will you admit you can't do everything well and farm out some of your work?

I know others can put guilt trips on us—husbands on wives, children on their parents, even friends on friends. But I say, Let them think what they want—I still need time for myself. I need to give myself permission to develop my own interests without feeling guilty for the time spent.

Learning to Receive
Suzanne Manthei

It is often difficult to ask for help. We may feel that no one else can accomplish the task the way we could, we may not want to inconvenience others, or we may feel too unworthy to be served. All these reasons are based on pride, and pride has no place in Christ's body. The following are four suggestions to help us put aside self-sufficiency:

Reach out. More people would help if they knew there was a problem. Sometimes we have to let our friends, family, or church know we need help.

Don't dismiss an offer to help. Most people want to help, but don't want to interfere. They may remark, "Call me if there's anything I can do." Pay attention to these comments. When they come, don't brush them aside—discuss them further. Be open to new suggestions; they may be answers from God.

Be content with what you're given. We all have known people who either seem to be habitually asking for help or abusing it: "Since you asked, can you keep my kids for four days next week?" or, "Can I borrow $400 to fix my car?"

Allow the person who helps you to set limits on what she can offer. If she is pressured to give more help than she is able, resentment may develop. Don't worry if she can't give you all the help you need—God will supply exactly the right measure in the right time.

Receive from God. God is a loving father who wants to take care of his children. When we realize he often gives through his people, we can understand he is still the source of our help. As we learn both to give *and* receive, the body of Christ functions the way God intended—through mutual support and encouragement.

From Today's Christian Woman
(November/December 1991)

Be Good to Yourself
Elizabeth Cody Newenhuyse

The issue of finding private time is deeper than merely finding physical solitude. Recently I was on the phone with a friend, almost in tears from exhaustion due to a pressing professional deadline and family illness. She listened sympathetically and said, "You need to do something good for *yourself* every day. Buy yourself a bouquet of carnations. Take a bubble bath. Get a haircut. Something *just* for you."

I mumbled a few words of agreement, then went home, read my daughter a story, gave her a bath, picked up the house, and watched television. Then, as I fell into bed, it occurred to me I hadn't done a single thing for myself that evening.

The reason: It's very difficult for me to do something that benefits no one *but* me—something like sitting on the porch to enjoy a spring dusk. How can I ignore the clamor of my house "yelling at me," in the apt phrase of a colleague?

And I know I'm not alone. I suspect many women, especially Christians, feel this way. After all, aren't we here to serve and to sacrifice? While we may *need* some time away from the demands of family and work, we've somehow programmed our minds to think we *shouldn't* want that. *Self* is a dirty word— unbiblical, hedonistic, an idol worshiped by secular culture. Or is it?

When I am exhausted, depleted by the clamor of the "cast of thousands" my life seems to include, I am of little good to God. Too tired to pray, to serve, to connect, to hear. God will get through to me eventually. But why make him yell?

Not long ago I was home alone for most of the day. I did all those things I love to do but seldom have time for: to leisurely read the paper, to rearrange the knickknacks, to talk to the parakeets, or to enjoy a cup of tea.

After dusk had fallen, my family returned and I greeted them gladly. Absence, or at least a break, *can* make the heart grow fonder. It's when you start living out of one another's pockets that things begin to grate. That's one reason it's essential to give yourself some time off.

We need to remember too, Jesus' injunction to love our neighbor *as ourself.* Jesus isn't talking about narcissistic adoration. Rather, he is encouraging us to *care* for ourselves—our own bodies, our minds, our spirits—in the same manner God cares for us.

What does this "caring for myself" mean as a wife, mother, and working woman who spends most of her time meeting someone else's expectations? It means sometimes it's okay to put myself first. Moms get leftover time as surely as we take the heel of bread. We can only relax when everyone is tended to, everything picked up.

But God thinks we're important too—not some second-class citizens in his creation. We're his. He made us, not to rush around in an exhausted frenzy, but to serve him and enjoy him.

From Today's Christian Woman
(May/June 1991)

Make It Happen

1. To better understand why private time is important, ask yourself, What is included in a life I respect? Do balance, variety, pacing, and peace enter the answer? Why do I think that life has value? Write out and reflect upon your answers.

2. If you find your mind spinning out of control when you do have some time to yourself, consider carrying a notebook to help you organize your thoughts.

3. Meditate on 1 Thessalonians 4:11,12 and Psalm 37:7 on the value of leading a quiet, peaceful inner life.

4. Look for holes in your life, for pockets that could be fuller and make you a more well-rounded person. When was the last time you had fun or did something just you enjoyed? If it's been more than a month, block off a morning on your calendar that's just for you. Then keep your eyes open for opportunities to invest that time wisely.

5. Read one of the Gospels and note how Christ used his time. Did he achieve a balance of time alone to replenish his spirit with his demanding work on earth? Look for other clues on how Christ led a balanced life.

Chapter 9

SHOULD I DOWNSCALE
MY CAREER?
Mary Whelchel

ine years ago, after a successful corporate career, which included working for IBM, I chose to pursue an open door God had given me for a radio ministry. I also opted to become a self-employed business trainer, so I could control when and how much I worked. Downscaling at this point in my career meant giving up a good position—one I had worked toward for years—and a lucrative salary. But the trade-off of being able to pursue new goals far outweighed these factors.

For the past three decades, women have been fed a subtle message: To be considered truly intelligent, ambitious, and successful, you need to take a career to the top. I learned firsthand how wrong this message is, and, thankfully, more women, Christian and non-Christian alike, are beginning to recognize its deception. As they discover that their identity does not depend on business success, and that often a full-fledged career doesn't bring the fulfillment they thought it would, or it has cost too much in terms of family relationships or service to the Lord, they too are choosing to downscale their careers.

Should I Downscale?

How do you know if you should leave the fast track you're on and pursue your goals at a slower pace, or perhaps pursue a different set of goals altogether? The first step is to pray and seek God's guidance. Working women are some of the busiest people in the world, so it's easy for us to shortchange our relationship with the Lord. But unless we're spending time with him on a daily basis, we can't really know his mind and hear him talk to us.

I'll admit I have to work at this discipline of spending time with the Lord. I'm a very project-oriented person, so when it comes time for my daily devotional hour, my mind says, You ought to be doing something. There's so much to do. Getting up early to spend quiet time with the Lord every morning takes commitment and discipline. But I know if I don't make that my top priority, I can't hear his voice when I have choices, and sometimes I won't even see the choices.

Flexing to Fit

Women want and need flexibility in their jobs. For that reason, I predict more women will become entrepreneurs—especially in fields that are service-oriented. I see women building smaller companies and concentrating their energies on opportunities that can be more easily adapted to their changing needs.

—Judith

Conquering Financial Fears

As we consider the Lord's guidance in our decision to downscale our careers, we also need to get down to the nuts and bolts of the issue—namely financial concerns. Can you survive on less than you currently earn? How much less?

Many women don't even consider downscaling an option because their current salary barely keeps pace with their standard of living. Typically, though, our lifestyles are cushioned with many luxuries we could learn to live without. Sorting out your wants from your needs is an important factor in working through the practical issues of downscaling. If you're willing to relinquish some of the unnecessary expenses that keep you slave to your paycheck, you may find you have more financial freedom than you thought.

Drawing a Road Map

Before you make a move toward downscaling, you need to develop a budget. Determine how much income you currently live on, how much you'd be willing to cut back, and what expenses you can do without to reach your goal. Remember, downscaling isn't something you can do overnight. It may take several years to get your finances in order, to pay off bills or sell your home and move to a more affordable one.

Welcome Home

Now that I'm older, I'm realizing it's okay to move out of the fast lane. I no longer feel the need to work every day from nine to five. I've spent over forty years financially preparing for the day when I can enjoy a more tranquil lifestyle, and I love it! It is okay to stay home; to operate at a less hectic pace. I've invested years in developing my home—I have a wonderful library and collection of music, and many dear friends with whom I can enjoy it. It's refreshing to spend time at home rather than chasing after something that doesn't exist.

—Luci

Not long ago I received a letter from a successful career woman who for the last six years knew that God wanted her to leave her current job and use her talents for one year in Christian work. She started saving her money six years ago when God spoke to her. And she wrote, "I've got enough money to tide me over for a year. I just resigned from my job."

She was headed for a one-year mission assignment overseas. She admitted this move wasn't easy, but she was ready to go. "I don't know what God has for me when I get back. I doubt I'll ever find another job like this one, but that's okay." She had heard God's voice and immediately made long-term plans so she would be able to follow him when the time came.

Our generation wants immediate results. But, as this woman's situation illustrates, major intentional lifestyle changes don't happen instantly. Often it takes careful financial planning.

As you go about your lifestyle changes, it helps to keep Romans 12:2 in mind: "Do not conform any longer to the pattern of this world, but be transformed by the renewing of your mind. Then you will be able to test and approve what God's will is—his good, pleasing and perfect will."

Jesus said you can't serve both God and money. About six years ago I read *The Challenge of the Disciplined Life: Christian Reflections on Money, Sex, and Power* by Richard J. Foster (HarperSanFrancisco). I soon realized how many of my decisions and priorities were controlled by money, as well as how much anxiety I have about money, or rather the fear of not having enough.

In fact, just this morning, I was sitting at my desk mulling over a financial matter and I thought, *If I had a major sickness or catastrophe, my retirement money would be gone in a flash. I'm single and no one is committed to taking care of me.* For a moment I panicked. But then I reminded myself I have a God who said he knows what I need and will supply it.

The major hurdle I had to jump before deciding to downscale was to stop looking to money for my security. I had to wean myself from wanting the security of working for a large company, from the power of money. In fact, early in my career, when I wasn't really walking with the Lord, I never would have had the confidence to downscale.

But walking by faith is something you learn by doing. You try it and say, Well, God got me through last year. He can get me through this year. Downscaling can be a wonderful step of faith, forcing you to learn to trust God in new ways that would never happen otherwise.

Forever Eyes

One thing that has helped me adjust to a downscaled career is to look at my world through what I call "forever eyes." I must look at life with a long-term perspective, and for a Christian, that means eternity.

Some day I'm going to have to stand in front of God and give an answer for how I've used my resources—my money, time, talents, abilities, home, and body. I'll have to report to Jesus why I made the choices I did. What would I answer if Jesus says, "You spent all this energy and time trying to make a lot of money and then when you got the money you bought a bigger house and more clothes."

I've come to realize it's not so important how comfortably I live here on earth. It's much more important to know that someday I'll be able to say, "Jesus, it was your house, your body, your mind, your money. I simply tried to be a good steward."

When I look at life through "forever eyes," I know careers are not eternal. God is not giving rewards for how high I climb a corporate ladder, although I do believe he wants Christians to do their work with excellence. And certainly he plans for some of us to climb the career ladder to the top so that we can witness to those who are there. In the end, God will hold me responsible for how I use the opportunities he gives me.

When the Going Gets Tough

When I first started my ministry and began the process of downscaling, I was scared to death. The ministry was growing and I wasn't sure what I was getting into.

I remember sitting down with my Bible and saying, "Lord, I will not take another step until I have a verse I can hang onto when times are tough, when I want to give up." It so happened that Isaiah 50 was on my reading schedule that day and verses four and seven stood out.

"The Sovereign LORD has given me an instructed tongue, to know the word that sustains the weary. . . . Because the Sovereign LORD helps me, I will not be disgraced. Therefore have I set my face like flint, and I know I will not be put to shame."

Those verses have carried me through many days when money wasn't there, when I felt totally incapable and incompetent, when I didn't get people's approval, and when I felt tired and discouraged. Many times I've clung to the promise that he will not allow me to be disgraced. In fact, that passage is now framed and hangs above my desk as a continued reminder and source of encouragement.

If you've got any fears (and we all do) or any doubts about scaling back your career, just tell God, "I know that your word is what will sustain me. I need a verse. I need a passage that I can cling to when the times get tough."

It also helps to have friends who will support you during this transition. I have several encouragers, both family and friends, who many times have confirmed their belief in my choice to downscale my career and step out in faith.

Never Say Never

Several years ago I was living a life where my self-esteem was based on what I achieved and how much I owned. I remember reading an article that listed women's salaries. At that time my pay ranked in the upper 5 percent among women, and I thought, "You have arrived." For a day I strutted around feeling special. But at night, that glow of being in the top 5 percent wore off as I lay there alone without even the Lord to share my accomplishments.

Ten years ago I came back to a close walk with the Lord after a ten-year detour, and the difference in my life is amazing. The loss of income, prestige, or power that went with downscaling are more than offset by the joy and peace of knowing God is using my small ministry to encourage and help many others who struggle in their work.

Today I sometimes take the peace I feel about life for granted. I always ask God to remind me what it was like when I had no peace, when my sense of satisfaction only lasted a short time. I don't want to ever forget that empty feeling.

Since I surrendered my life to the Lord, I'm no longer possessed by this drive to prove I'm a cutting-edge, powerful, successful businesswoman. Downscaling was God's plan for me, and it has brought great joy. If it is in God's plan for you, trust him with the details and he will become your security blanket.

Make It Happen

1. As you downscale, make it a daily habit to commit your choice to the Lord. We'd like to say, "God gave me the confidence to downscale and ever since things have been fine." But it's not that simple. Realize it is a daily decision to keep your life aligned with God's plan for you and not the world's expectations.

2. Look for evidences of a growing trust in God. Remember, it's gradual and can sometimes go unnoticed. But did he provide for you last week, last month? Have you really made an effort to depend on him?

3. Ask the Lord for a specific verse that will enable you to make it through the tough times. Consider framing it and putting it on your desk or in another visible area where you'll read it every day.

Chapter 10

HOW CAN I BE CONFIDENT THE CHOICES I MAKE TODAY WON'T LEAD TO REGRETS TOMORROW?
Judith Briles

ouldn't it be great if our lives were a video tape? Then when we made a mistake or a bad decision, we'd simply pop it in, rewind past the bad spots, and tape over it. I'll admit, there are events in my life where I'd like to go back and change the outcome, but I can't. God created a world that goes forward. Yet I think women especially try to rewind the tape with two simple words—*if only*.

"If only my schedule had been more flexible when the kids were young." "If only I had checked out this business venture more thoroughly." The "if only" list is endless. What we need to remember, though, is that as women today we are managing our lives in ways our mothers never dreamed. We don't have the role models of a former generation. In my mother's time, she could look back at her mother's life and most likely the choices and responsibilities she made would be quite similar to her mother's. Now we have a whole new arena in which to make choices, both good and bad—the work world. And, for the most part, we can't look back to see how our mothers or grandmothers dealt with these choices. They didn't have them.

When you're doing something new, something that doesn't

fit the mold, doubts and regrets are bound to creep in. You might wonder, Did I do the right thing? Take some comfort in the fact you will make mistakes, you will blow it. All of us do. And for some women, the choices they make may even be subject to public scrutiny. Whenever you have a high profile and you go against the grain, the media tends to analyze and write about you more.

I have several friends in their forties who have not married yet. Now they look at their peers with families and wonder, Did this opportunity pass me by? Should I have jumped off the career path to have a family? My response to them is, Who knows? Women in the nineties will fill a variety of different roles. Some will have families, some won't. Some will take their careers to the top, others won't. Some will be featured in *Time* magazine, others won't.

Keep On Movin'

Some mornings I get up and feel blue or frustrated about something. I think, Luci, you've got twelve hours ahead of you. You can lie in bed all day, mope, and feel sorry for yourself. You've got the freedom to do that. Or you can get up and go out. You've got options and you can choose. On occasion I have chosen to lie in bed all day, but at the end of the day I didn't feel one bit better—the problem hadn't gone away. Yet when I choose to be active, the problem may still exist, but I'm better able to handle it.

—Luci

Although it sounds pat, I honestly believe if something is meant to be, it will be. The decisions we make in life, whether made consciously or unconsciously, are truly in someone else's hands—God's.

As you compare yourself to others or to the media's perception of reality (and each of us does at one time or the other) it may appear you made wrong choices. Soon you fill your mind with regrets and "if onlys." The sad result is a heart and mind closed to other paths the Lord may be leading you down.

Look in the Mirror

If your regrets and doubts are mounting, you owe it to yourself to look for the answers to why you feel the way you do.

Are you truly feeling regret for some of the life decisions you've made? Or are you listening to everyone but yourself and God? Sometimes I think we feel regret more out of conditioning than from a true sense of loss.

To weed out some of these conditioned responses, learn to dialogue with yourself, whether it is through meditation, prayer, or even going for a walk. Sometimes when I drive, I talk to myself and I'm amazed at the revelations I have.

Bear in mind that God is always your partner. He listens—and answers. There have been many times the answers have not been to my liking. But always when I look back, I realize they were right. I have learned to trust.

Calling for Help

When it comes to decisions and choices about work and life, expect yourself to go back and forth emotionally. Did I do the right thing? Did I make a mistake? As soon as a hard time hits, you may go into panic mode. Turn your anxiety over to the Lord. Don't be afraid to cry, "Help! I can't do this!" He's there waiting for us. He says, "I'm going to walk you through this, you won't drown. I want you to learn to trust in me."

—Mary

If you're feeling a sense of regret about a career decision, it helps to take into account a growing trend among working women—pursuing multiple careers, or sequencing, which allows you to integrate other interests and responsibilities, such as parenting, into your career path. Decades ago, people were trained in a skill and stayed with a job until retirement. Today, I see more and more women taking time to prioritize based on their particular stage in life and then making career moves according to their needs and goals at the time. The result is women are no longer tied to a single career path. We are free to take time off to raise a family or to move from one career into another. With options like these, regrets or poor decisions become stepping stones to the future, not an anchor to the past.

Failure Leads to Success

Never did I envision my life taking the course it has—from stockbroker to financial planner to author to a speaker on women's issues. But I've learned to be open, to see the opportunities in different situations. I may not have succeeded in the trading world to the degree I would have liked. And, admittedly, it did take time for me to view the end of that career as an opportunity to grow in a new direction rather than feel as though I had failed. In fact, working through that passage in my life taught me a lot about the way women handle failure and regrets. My own experience—and research bears this out—is that women tend to identify personally with failure. Men, on the other hand, tend to see failure as a learning experience, not a reflection of their character. Understanding this difference gives us better insight into why we women sometimes wrestle with regret over decisions and choices.

When a man experiences a failure, say his business fails or loses money, he's more inclined to look at the event as a growing opportunity. He asks himself, What have I learned? What's the next step?

However, when it comes to either a private or a public failure, women are more inclined to view themselves as flawed or incompetent. A poor choice is a direct reflection of a woman's character. Instead of viewing regrets or failures as mistakes from which we can learn, most women tend to view them as negatives—embarrassing moments to be hidden for fear others might think poorly of us because of them.

Oddly enough, while women typically tend to offer empathy and compassion easily, when it comes to failure, we aren't as quick to extend a hand to our sisters or ourselves. When I was in the midst of a very bad business situation, the support wasn't there for me. The feeling among my female colleagues was that I was responsible for the mess. It hurt. I needed support as I spent years unraveling a former partner's misdeeds.

While I would like to see women support one another better through business and personal failures, I think one of the reasons we don't is because we were raised to avoid risk. We were encouraged to stay away from situations that would bring attention to us, or that might humiliate or embarrass those we were with. Boys, on the other hand, were encouraged to take risks, to experience failure. By avoiding risk, many of us were deprived of the opportunity to feel failure and learn appropriate responses to it.

Moving On

Failure and the regrets that follow are very painful. When your personal life or business is public knowledge, you must come to grips with it—validate it, confront it, and then move on. But if the failure is private—say, your family life is a disaster or you are bordering on financial bankruptcy—we often don't have the opportunity to bring this type of failure to a formal close. If that's the case, get talking. Healing begins when you start verbalizing what you feel.

I've found when I speak to women's groups about the failures or regrets I've experienced, inevitably someone says to me, "I can't believe you're telling us this. You look like you've always been successful. It helps to know you've failed, too."

So find a good friend, an objective listener, and talk out your regrets or feelings of failure. Confronting failures or people you may have failed is tough. But it's essential. It's a critical step in the process of forgiveness. An apology, if it is warranted, can move you beyond the point of failure too. Likewise, confronting someone who has hurt you or in some way failed you gives you a chance to tell them how their words or actions made you feel. It lets them know you are aware of their actions.

Whether you're working through your own failures or the pain of someone having let you down, you need to move on after you've confronted the situation. That's the hard part. You may want to ask the Lord for help in overcoming the negative feelings that are holding you back. A simple prayer like, "Lord give me strength to move on," will keep you moving in the right direction.

In my research regarding confidence among business women, the common denominator among America's most successful women in the workplace was their failure rate. Successful women took risks and didn't fear failure. In fact, for them, failure and success went hand in hand. And as I talked with these women, I found that being able to forgive themselves was what moved them beyond failure and toward success.

Learning Forgiveness

But how do you move from failure to forgiveness—especially when we as women tend to be so unforgiving of ourselves? The first step is to look at the standard you've set for yourself. If perfection is your goal, you're setting yourself up for failure.

Second, remember if you make a mistake it doesn't mean you as a person are not good. I know of a woman who went into business with another graphic designer only to see the business fail miserably. Thousands of dollars were lost. The true cause of the failure was her partner, yet this woman was certain if only she worked harder, the business would succeed. For nearly a year, she worked 18 to 20 hour days—anything she could do to somehow improve the situation. But it wasn't fixable.

Only after talking with others did she realize it was her partner's poor business sense that undid their company. Once she was able to relinquish responsibility for the failure, she was able to move on.

So What . . .

If you're having a hard time moving beyond feelings of regret, ask yourself, What happened? Retrace the steps that brought you where you are today. Then tell yourself, It just didn't work out. Take a moment to step back from the situation and look at it objectively. Ask yourself, So what if I don't do this or that? Most likely, the earth will not stop.

Presently, I'm in a situation where I'm so behind on a personal book deadline I'm thinking this book is a big mistake. But I have to tell myself, Stop that kind of thinking, you are sabotaging your ideas. When I look at the situation objectively, I know the reason I'm behind is because I go through periods where my creativity is blocked. When I jump this hurdle, the book will go fast. In my heart, as I listen to its voice, I know this is true. So I called the publisher and said, "This is what is happening with me right now." He said, "Fine, let's reschedule." The earth didn't stop.

Now, I could have spent the day mentally beating myself up, berating myself, and letting myself know how dumb and incompetent I am. But that is counterproductive. Positive self-talk will always take you further than negative self-talk.

I've learned this again and again from my speaking engagements. I usually receive evaluations from the audience. Three or four out of every hundred may say "no sense of humor, crummy stories, took too long, can't stand the dress." Which ones did I concentrate on? The negative ones. Now I note the negative comments then toss them out. I keep the ones that say, "loved the stories, loved the humor, I can relate, you changed my life." I have learned that I will never please everyone, even those I love. Neither will you.

Say Yes to Risks

Because we have choices, we will have regrets. No matter what choices you've made, you can't go back and do it over again. Rather than wallow in self-pity, ask yourself, What am I doing right now? Maybe you weren't the ideal spouse or mother, or you weren't as involved in your community as you would have liked. But certainly there are many things you've done well. It's helped me to view feelings of regret as turning points.

As a parent, one of my philosophies has been: Love your children enough to let them fail. Let them make mistakes and learn. The same adage can apply to us, too: Love yourself enough to let yourself fail.

We all have the opportunity to make changes. The question is, "How are you going to maximize that opportunity?" As soon as you learn to say, What's the worst thing that can happen? taking risks becomes easier. Your choices become clearer. You can meet those feelings of regret head-on, and you'll have the assurance that each decision and its consequences will send you in the direction the Lord wants you to follow. It is called living.

Make It Happen

1. We've all made poor decisions, but surprisingly the outcome isn't always bad. Take a sheet of paper and write down all you've learned from a particular disaster, failure, or mistake you made. What did it tell you about your values, your priorities, your relationships? Learn to look at a decision you might have regretted as a learning opportunity.

2. Read James 1:5, Proverbs 13:20, Psalm 111:10, Proverbs 2:6. As you go about making choices, remember to ask God for wisdom to make the best ones.

3. Consider forming a lunch-time round-table discussion group with several co-workers or friends—people who share common concerns, hopes, even dreams. Meet monthly to touch base on the issues and problems each of you is facing. Encourage each participant to share how she has handled certain situations and what she's learned along the way. One point to remember: the objective is to share, not to pass judgment on others.

Chapter 11

HOW INVOLVED CAN I EXPECT TO BE IN MY CHURCH?
Judith Briles

erhaps your work is leaving little time for church. Or maybe you're wondering if you should take on a Sunday school class though it will mean less time for your family. How do we find that balance between the many daily demands we face and our desire to be active in the church?

The first step is realizing that church represents but one facet of our relationship with Christ. There's no question our involvement and attendance at church are critical to our spiritual growth and to the well-being of the family of God. Yet sometimes I think we worry too much about the number of hours we put in there, as if this were a barometer of our commitment to the Lord.

At times I've been deeply involved in church. I've also had to say, "I need a break." There was even a time in my life when I was still practicing my faith but remained nearly dormant in my church involvement because I was looking for the right fit of my talents, needs, and personality. When I finally found a smaller church that had the intimacy I sought, I quickly began to take on responsibilities. I became an elder. With my knowledge of finances, I also was elected chairperson of the Stewardship Committee.

Unfortunately, what began as a good use of my talents soon turned into an ugly mess when someone from my committee leaked confidential information about individual pledging commitments to members of the congregation. Our church became divided, and I felt caught in the middle of the turmoil. I wanted to quit, yet I really believed God put me in that position for a purpose, despite the pain.

I remember pleading with God one night to get me out of the mess. All of a sudden, an incredible sensation came over me. It felt as if Jesus' arms were around me, holding me, and I heard him say, "You have to be there."

Master of Motivation

I'm always amazed at what a great manager the Lord is. He motivates each of us to serve him by giving us gifts. And then when we use our gifts for his glory, we feel privileged for the opportunity to serve. One of my gifts is to make the Bible practical and relatable. And I've learned that when the Lord gives us gifts, we can be confident he'll direct where to use them.

—Mary

I stuck it out for three years, in which time our divided church family was made whole again with the help of an interim minister. When our new permanent pastor arrived, I knew my time was up as Stewardship Chair. I had done everything from decorating myself as a Christmas tree, to talking about giving, to scraping together funds for the new pastor's home. I was exhausted. Thus I learned one of the first, and possibly most important, lessons about church involvement: know when enough is enough. I needed time to worship again.

Being Open to New Gifts

Many times (and I'm certainly not immune) we jump into things without thinking them through. It's so simple to say, "Sure, I'll do it." But what we really should do is consult God about our opportunities and commitments. Is this involvement truly his leading? Should I be doing it *now*?

Working women need to recognize that church is just one of the many parts in our relationship with God. Where we carry out our service to him and grow in faith will change from time to time. The most intimate, intense spiritual insights may not occur in a church pew on Christmas Eve. Instead it might be while you're alone driving, pleading with God, as I experienced.

Be open and flexible to how God is going to use you in his church. We tend to do those things we know best, but I encourage you to stretch and venture into new areas at times. Study the church bulletin. See what the needs are.

Natural By-product

Everyone's church involvement varies. To the degree God and the Holy Spirit open the door for ministry in which we feel comfortable and of service, we should be involved. God's word encourages us to assemble together. The nature and the amount of our involvement is a natural by-product of that encouragement.

—Luci

Too often we assume, That's not one of the gifts I've been given. I wonder is that really true? Not long ago I read about former Olympic gymnast Cathy Rigby's desire to sing. She had a horrible, screechy voice and she took lessons for three years. Her kids would hold their hands over their ears and beg her to stop. If you have seen the latest rendition of the play *Peter Pan*, Cathy's lessons served her well—she sounds great. A new gift!

Take the time to tune into yourself and how you work. What are your strongest skills? What are your talents? How can they be tied together in the framework of serving your church? When you're sorting out your interests also consider whether you work better on committees or as a solo practitioner. Just that alone will help you separate the many opportunities for involvement in church.

Likewise, what are some skills you would like to develop? Maybe you've always wanted to be a teacher yet your career or other commitments offer no opportunity to teach. The church is often an ideal place to try your hand at new skills.

As you become more active within the church, remember: you need to be honest with yourself and those who ask for your help. It's okay to say, "This is what I can do right now." When you're at your limit and have to say no, say so.

One technique I've used that eases some of the self-imposed guilt is to present an alternative. Be honest. Tell your fellow church member you can't help out with the food drive this month but you'll be happy to next month. Or consider offering a friend's name who is equally qualified to help and who you know has an open spot in her schedule. While you are offering options, you are also staying true to yourself—a critical factor in maintaining balance.

Staying true to yourself is always key whenever you're considering taking on new responsibilities. For instance, perhaps you want to volunteer your time at church, but you just can't take on a long-term commitment. If you're like me, frustration mounts when you never seem to be able to draw a line through an item on your endless to-do list. Short-term projects are a great way to gain a sense of accomplishment and closure. I know a woman who chaired a portion of the program for a women's retreat. It took three or four meetings over a three-month period, but when the retreat was finished, so was her obligation.

Wanting to Hide

What are some signs of overcommitment? If you find yourself saying, "I don't have time," followed by, "Everyone is pulling me in different directions—serve here, join this, support that," there's a good chance you'll feel the desire to drop out. Burnout is a sure sign that you may need just to worship each Sunday and retreat from other church activities, at least for a time.

Sometimes you have to say no to everything else and just attend services and tithe. If this is the case, it's essential that you let your fellow members be aware of your decision. Call them and say, "I'm overloaded right now, so for a time I'm just going to attend worship services. I want you to know I support what you're doing, but I just have to take a break right now."

Often during the summer, electrical brownouts occur

because utility services are overloaded, usually from air conditioning. When this happens, the electric companies tell their customers to cut back. Similarly, if you're feeling overloaded with church commitments, your "electricity" is likely to brown out. Cutting back temporarily may be the answer to restoring yourself back to full service.

———— ·❦· ————

Remember, serving your church at times requires nothing more than your attendance. The church needs your support, and that means your physical presence. Concepts and movements can fail or succeed by your very presence or lack of it.

God has given each of us a variety of talents and abilities, some of which we will use in a church setting. I've come to realize these gifts will be activated and used at different times throughout my life. Sometimes I'll be highly involved in my church, and at other times I'll know it's okay to simply attend church to be rejuvenated and nurtured in the Lord.

When we look at our commitments within the church, it becomes a question of stewardship—of ourselves, our time, our talents, our families. In serving our church, we can't afford to neglect ourselves, or our families. If we're not whole in body and soul, if we're running ourselves ragged, how can we possibly hope to be effective serving our church?

I don't think our Lord wants church to become another item on our to-do list. We can avoid that by learning to listen to ourselves and prayerfully accept responsibilities within the church. But above all, we need to remember what pleases the Lord most is our willingness to worship him always with a heart open to his leading.

Finding the Niche That Fits
Karen Dockrey

Do you feel you haven't found the right niche in your church for your gifts and interests? If you can't sew, play piano, or cross stitch, remember—women's ministries aren't limited to these activities. Let God guide you to discover the spiritual gifts he has given you and how he wants you to express them effectively. Here are some gifts you might have overlooked.

Wisdom. Wisdom is the ability to apply God's truth to everyday living. Women with wisdom give good advice, make the Bible clear, and focus on the things that count. In church you might find these persons as committee members or counselors.

Faith. Though all Christians have saving faith, those with the spiritual gift of faith have an extraordinary ability to trust God during times of intense trouble. They know without a doubt God is in control and he will get us through. They don't put others down for doubting or make them feel less spiritual. They simply believe God—and their confidence is contagious. Women with this gift pray for committees and councils, visit and pray for the sick, and uphold others when discouraged.

Teaching. Teachers make the Bible clear. They guide their students to discover God's truth for themselves and to live what they discover. The best teachers teach the age group they love. Some teach Sunday school, others lead home Bible studies.

Encouragement. Encouragers motivate others to live out their faith. They make you want to express your faith because they have confidence in you.

Encouragers direct departments, serve as nominating committee members, or say appreciative words to those who work hard.

Mercy. Those who show mercy care for the sick and needy without pity or a sense of duty. They meet needs because they care. Merciful people serve on benevolence committees, work with food pantries, or prepare meals in soup kitchens. A Bible verse that best describes these women might be Matthew 25:40; "I tell you the truth, whatever you did for one of the least of these brothers of mine, you did for me."

Leadership. Leaders guide groups of believers to grow in Christ. In the church, leaders take initiative rather than wait for someone else to start. They notice needs, recruit people to meet those needs, train them, and guide them.

Find your match. Read about spiritual gifts in Romans 12:3-8, Ephesians 4:1-13, and 1 Corinthians 12:4-11. Notice gifts that seem to jump off the page at you. Circle ones that touch your heart and talk with God about which ones he wants you to express and how. When you express the gifts God has given you, you'll make a difference in your church and community.

From Today's Christian Woman
(September/October 1989)

Make It Happen

1. List your current involvements and commitments at church. Consider each item and ask yourself: Do I truly enjoy this? Is this commitment a good match for my time, gifts, and energy? Am I involved out of a sense of guilt? Did I say yes to this involvement without clearly thinking it through? If you said yes to the last two questions then it's time to rethink your involvements and consider dropping those that are draining you. As it says in Ecclesiastes 4:6, "Better one handful with tranquility than two handfuls with toil and chasing after the wind."

2. If you are burned out with church involvements, consider finishing those commitments that are outstanding and then take a month off—do nothing but worship. Get back to a time where, as it says in Psalm 100:2, you can indeed "serve the LORD with gladness," not heaviness of heart.

3. Ask a friend at church or your pastor to help you assess what your strengths and interests are and how you can best serve your church. An objective third party can open your eyes to exciting new opportunities.

4. Leave your church involvement in the hands of God, trusting that he will direct you to a need that matches your time and talents. Bring your request before God in your daily prayers and ask that he keep you sensitive to his promptings.

Section 3

PUTTING CHRISTIAN CHARACTER TO WORK

**Y**our co-worker gets the promotion you wanted. Your emotions bristle as the boss takes his anger out on you. Your job seems particularly frustrating and unfulfilling. We've all experienced them—tough days and dilemmas that tax our reserves and test our character.

How do we handle ourselves when the going gets tough? How can we keep our Christian character intact when the inevitable stresses and challenges of the workplace seem so capable of tearing it away.

As Mary and Luci point out in the following section, allowing God's precepts to transform our human nature is not accomplished by a quick and easy 1-2-3 formula. More often than not, it takes a maturity and wisdom that can only be gained through trial and error. While the Lord offers us his wisdom in his Word, he also gives us a free will—and with that free will the potential to make mistakes. Nevertheless, he can lovingly use those mistakes to teach us valuable lessons.

In the following chapters, Luci and Mary share some very personal stories on how they learned to put Christian character to work—on good days *and* bad.

Chapter 12

SHOULD I SPEAK UP IF COMPANY PRACTICES GO AGAINST MY PERSONAL INTEGRITY?
Mary Whelchel

he other day I received a letter from a listener who described a sticky situation she had encountered at work. Her supervisor wanted her to change some figures on a proposal to improve a sales presentation. She knew that would be dishonest—and as a Christian she simply could not comply with such deception. She refused to alter the figures, knowing full well it would jeopardize the account, which, if they lost, would also directly affect her sales commission.

When she wrote me, the final outcome was still unknown. Would she lose her job? Would she damage her career? She didn't predict a happy ending for taking a stand against lying. But one thing she did know for certain—Jesus would have wanted her to say no. And added to that, she knew that Jesus would take care of her because she had done the right thing.

What do we do when our sense of right conflicts with the company's ethics? Is it better to say nothing when you realize that company practices go against Christian principles? Or do we boldly take a stand and voice our objections?

The answer is both. The challenge lies in knowing which path to take when.

Should I Speak Up?

Another listener wrote to me recently about a time when she attended a series of motivational seminars at her supervisor's request only to find the seminar content based on New Age principles. She found it difficult to participate in something so contrary to her faith. Finally, she told her manager she could no longer attend. She admitted in her letter that taking such a stand wouldn't help her career any. After all, her manager had planned the seminars. But she had to do what she felt was right.

Hold Firm

If sticking to your principles closes one door, I'm certain God will open another. I was once asked to write an article with a specific slant for a business women's magazine. I did my research only to find what the editors wanted me to write wouldn't be the truth. I said, "I'll either write this article the way the facts speak or I won't write it." I lost the assignment as well as a sizable fee when I could have used the money. Some time later I was asked by another company to write an article, which I did. The fee they paid me more than compensated for the loss I took on the first assignment.

—Judith

As Christians, the time to take a stand against unethical company procedures is when we are asked to participate in something that clearly goes against biblical mandates—whether directly or indirectly. That includes outright deception, like the experience the first woman I mentioned encountered, or participating in a seminar that unquestionably opposes Christian principles.

Any time an employer asks you to do something that compromises your beliefs, the answer should be no. You don't even need to pray about how to respond—it should be automatic. If you know the Word of God, it's clear how the Lord expects you to react in such circumstances. Jesus taught us to render to Caesar what is Caesar's, and to God what is God's. When our "Caesars" (an employer or co-worker) ask of us things that cause us to compromise what God requires of us, our priorities are clear. God comes first.

Now I'll agree, that doesn't make it any easier. After all,

when you do speak out, you can put your job on the line or run the risk of creating a rift between you and your supervisor. The woman who would not lie about the sales proposal was shaking the whole time she spoke to her supervisor. But as Christians, we cannot ask the question, How can I do the right thing without damaging my career? The essential questions instead are, What is the right thing to do? and, What does it mean to maintain my integrity?

You may be in a position where you can't do anything to save your career. In that case, you have to be prepared to say, "I'm going to do what's right with the knowledge that the consequences are in God's hands." The issue for Christians is not keeping our jobs, but instead keeping our integrity intact. And that means being willing to do whatever it takes to maintain our moral standards.

> ## Worth Talking About
>
> As long as we conduct ourselves with sincerity, professionalism, and tact, we have the right to speak up when company practices go against our integrity. It may not change the situation but at least we've accomplished three important things: made our preference known and why; caused others to think about the same issues; and enabled us to be true to ourselves.
>
> —Luci

If you are confident about the need to speak up, just as the two women were, then do so. But remember, the words we use in these situations can be just as important as the decision to speak out.

Avoid saying anything that sounds like you are the "good guy" and your supervisor or coworker is the "bad guy." Even using the sentence, "I can't participate because I'm a Christian," is not necessarily the wisest approach. "Being a Christian" has different meanings to different people. If you say, "I can't do this, I'm a Christian," you may get, "Well, I'm a Christian too, and I see no problem with it."

I strongly suggest keeping the focus on your personal beliefs in as nonjudgmental a way as possible. You could say, "This activity goes against *my* beliefs," or "*my* principles," or "*my* standards." Even if the issue involves New Age practices, still consider phrasing your objections as "This goes against my personal religious beliefs," rather than, "I'm a Christian."

Try using as gentle an approach as possible. Acknowledge that the issue is a personal one, that your reasons for not accommodating your supervisor are based on your principles and not because you don't want to be a team player. Don't be afraid to ask for your supervisor's understanding.

While gentleness is the best approach, at times a stronger approach is necessary. Take, for instance, the simple yet common practice of being asked to say the boss isn't in when indeed he or she is. To do this is lying. Instead, I advise people to say, "He, or she, is not available," which accomplishes the same purpose without deception. There are some supervisors, however, who demand a lie be told. But that's no reason to back down, as a friend of mine showed me. With a little creativity and a firm stand, her message came through loud and clear.

She worked for a man who insisted she screen his calls and tell those he didn't want to talk to that he wasn't in. "I can't do that because it isn't true," she told him. "I can only say you're not in when you're actually out of the office." Ultimately her way won out, and he came up with his own solution. It was a bit of an office joke, but every time he wanted her to say he wasn't in the office, he would walk completely outside of the building.

Granted, my friend has a lot of spunk and could pull off something like this. But because she wouldn't compromise, her solid integrity earned her the boss's respect. He was willing to accommodate her wishes.

If your supervisor is insistent on your doing something against your personal beliefs, let your supervisor know immediately that you have a problem with whatever you're being asked to do. Be up front about where you stand. "I try to be truthful in everything I say, and I'm very uncomfortable with being asked to say something which is not true. As a matter of fact, I just can't do it. But I'm hopeful we can work this out to our mutual satisfaction."

I remember the story a business associate told me when he

was asked to lie for his boss. He simply said, "If I were to lie *for* you, how could you ever be sure that I wouldn't lie *to* you?" I'm sure that made his boss think twice.

Another word of advice to keep in mind—make sure your emotions are in check before expressing your feelings about a situation that compromises your integrity. It's not uncommon to feel a sense of anger when you're pressured to do something you know is wrong. Give yourself time to gather your thoughts and prepare your speech. You'll be less likely to say something you'll later regret or wish you had said in private to your supervisor.

When to Keep Quiet

In almost any organization, co-workers will often behave contrary to our Christian standards. While their behavior may not infringe on us personally, we sometimes wonder, should I speak up? If we see a supervisor routinely promise favors to clients to get their business, knowing full well he can't possibly keep those promises, do we call him on the carpet with his behavior? Is there a moral directive that says we should report a co-worker who cheats on his expense account or takes home office supplies?

More often than not the answer will be no. I don't believe Christians are required to be the company "police officers," nor is it necessary to take a verbal stand on every unethical business practice we witness. Although at times Jesus did blow the whistle, he didn't point out the sin in every person he met.

Remember, everyone is accountable for their own actions. Now this doesn't mean we should never take the risk of confronting, but it does mean we should weigh those risks and consequences carefully. In those situations that aren't clearly black and white, the foremost action to take is to pray. A Christian who goes to the Lord and says, "I want to do the right thing but I'm not sure what that is," will get his direction on how to respond. It can also be helpful to get some godly counsel from someone you trust outside the company.

—⊷⊶—

We live in an imperfect world and that means we work in an imperfect business world as well. In a society motivated by self, it shouldn't surprise us to see unethical behavior. Even in the best of companies, you will find dishonest people.

Take, for instance, the misuse of the company's long distance phone service. You might know that certain employees are abusing this service—making personal calls at the company's expense. Should you report it? Unless you are the manager I would say no. Besides, in situations like this, many times management is aware of the abuse and often is part of it.

Your responsibility is to make sure *you* are not misusing the phone service and *your* principles are not being compromised.

—⊷⊶—

While we aren't called to be the company police squad, that doesn't mean we're supposed to just sit back and watch unethical practices being acted out. It's important to remember that, depending on your position, you may be able to influence company policy in the right direction—one that is based on Christian principles. After all, Christian principles work—no matter what the setting. If a company doesn't choose to abide by such principles, they pay a price at some later date. Cheating may work for a time, but it is eventually exposed. Favoritism may make some co-workers happy, but before long it erodes staff morale.

If you can be involved at the policy level, you will be doing your company a huge favor to promote ethical standards. Often companies base policies on the short term—what can get them a buck now. But they fail to realize it's the long-term policies that make or break them. When you do have the opportunity to offer suggestions on company policy, use the directives of what is right and what is best as set forth in the Bible.

For example, you might suggest that telephone standards be established and put in writing, to improve the image of the company and customer service. You could even volunteer to write a draft of the standards and get a committee together to refine them. You don't have to be a manager to make a suggestion.

126

It's surprising, but to put God's mechanics in operation you don't need to be loud. You simply have to build your credibility, then work through the system to make a change. Don't look for change overnight. It's usually a gradual process, but as Christians I think we have a definite responsibility to influence policy.

Tiptop Integrity

Standing up for what's right carries no weight unless you strive for honesty in every aspect of your job. Are your expense accounts accurate? Is your time card correct? Do you take only the lunch and break time allotted? Go the extra mile to establish that your own personal integrity is squeaky clean in the big *and* little areas. People notice that.

Recently I went out for dinner with a longtime friend who is not a believer, and he insisted on paying the bill. He then proceeded to hand me the check stub and said, "Here, charge this to your expense account." I refused. Even though I was on a business trip and no one but myself and my friend would know the truth, I would not charge something to my expense account that I didn't pay for.

It was tempting. I could have rationalized and found ways to make it seem okay. But the bottom line was, I did not pay for dinner and I had no right to be reimbursed. My friend acted as though I was foolish, but at least he knew I practiced what I preached.

If we fail in the little areas, we can't hope to have a credible witness in the big picture. If you say to a supervisor, "I can't lie," yet continue to take long lunch hours, come in late, or fail to put in a full day of work, your stand will have very little impact.

Recently at a conference I was talking about fatal flaws—that part of our personality that is a stumbling block. After I finished, a woman came up to me and said, "My fatal flaw is lying. I lie when I don't have to. I lie to make myself look better."

She was really struggling with this. I gave her some verses to memorize. Then I advised her to immediately go back to any person she lies to from this moment on, apologize, and set the record straight. If she will start studying God's Word about dishonesty and not allow herself to get by with even the smallest lie, I know she can break that bad habit and, in the process, establish a strong testimony for the Lord. We can't be perfect all the time, but when we blow it, we need to go back and make amends.

Expect It to Be Tough

In this world we will feel persecuted when we stand up for what is right. If we don't experience a few tough times, we need to ask, Is my life really demonstrating Jesus Christ?

A verse that has helped guide me is Proverbs 21:21: "He who pursues righteousness and love finds life, prosperity and honor." This is an excellent motto for working Christians.

What does it mean to pursue righteousness? It simply means doing the right thing—in any situation—and doing it in love. Our job is to take God's principles and apply them to the situations we face. And we need to do so without worrying about being fired or missing out on a promotion.

———

While we'd like to think our stand for what is right speaks volumes, we need to remember there are two ways those who see our light shine in the workplace can respond. In 2 Corinthians 2:15-16 it says, "For we are to God the aroma of Christ among those who are being saved and those who are perishing. To the one we are the smell of death; to the other, the fragrance of life."

Some will appreciate our seeking out what's right and like what we stand for. Yet others may say, "That's not for me." If your lifestyle is pure, it may be convicting to a person in darkness. And they may not want the light of your life to illuminate the lack of purity in their own.

Be prepared for negative reactions. It would be nice if everyone applauded your moral standards and admired your ethical principles, but don't count on it. At times, the reaction may be the exact opposite. Your life may create an atmosphere that makes others uncomfortable.

When you find someone is reacting negatively to your personal stand or lifestyle, I encourage you to surround the situation with prayer. Know God is on your side and work at keeping your words kind and loving. Also, be consistent in your behavior toward that co-worker or supervisor. Be the same person you were before you took a stand on an issue and then don't continue to bring the issue up. You've spoken out about how you feel and now it's time to move on.

It may cause friction for a while. But as Christian working women, we are to shine—not condemn or isolate ourselves from those who don't live by our standards. And we can pursue righteousness in the workplace because our confidence rests in the Lord—not in what others think of our actions.

"Just Sign It"
Debra Petrosky

"Carol, here's the inspection document for that rush order. I need it for a one o'clock deadline. I'm sure we met quality control standards—although we didn't have time for any final checking. Could you just sign it?"

Your supervisor has just asked you to lie—the inspection had not been done yet your signature would indicate otherwise. What do you do? Should you sign the paper just this once, hoping it won't happen again? How can you keep from violating your convictions without being perceived as "holier-than-thou"?

Here are some guidelines:

• When starting a new job, be prepared to take a stand right away. If you do something unethical once and you want to bow out gracefully on a subsequent conflict, your boss may say, "Well, you signed it last week when I asked. Why can't you sign it now?"

• Respect your supervisor's position regardless of his integrity and honesty. Let him know you're working to make him successful *before* a conflict occurs.

• State your own conviction in a nonaccusatory way. "Mr. Thomas, I realize you have a deadline to meet. But I have a conviction against lying, and I can't sign that document." That's far better than saying, "I can't believe you're asking me to falsify our inspection!"

• Suggest an alternative. "Mr. Thomas, I'm required to sample ten out of every one hundred widgets. Why don't I work through lunch so I can sign the inspection report for you by one o'clock?"

• Finally, make sure your work is impeccable. If you're tardy, sloppy, or behind in your duties, your supervisor will spot your hypocrisy. Integrity is a rare commodity in the workplace. Your relationship with Christ, displayed in practical ways, will cause others to notice. And you'll have a perfect opportunity to share your faith.

From Today's Christian Woman
(January/February 1991)

Make It Happen

1. Realize that your first and primary responsibility is to do your job and do it well. Are you meeting all the requirements of your position? If someone were watching your behavior on the job what would they think of you as an employee? As a Christian, does your personal sense of integrity match up with your actions?

2. Locate those areas that might be considered your "fatal flaws." Are they damaging your integrity? Starting today, make a dedicated effort to remedy the situation. Map out what three steps you plan on taking to improve your image at work. When you've overcome one area, move to the next. Don't try to improve too many areas at once. It's impossible and only leads to a sense of failure rather than success.

3. Pray consistently for those co-workers who haven't accepted Christ in their lives, for those who bend the rules, and for those who let their moral standards slide when the pressures of the workplace are great. When you see a co-worker making decisions that are selfishly based, pray that their eyes might be opened. And pray that your compassion for your co-workers will grow.

Chapter 13

IS IT EVER OKAY TO LOSE MY TEMPER AT WORK?
Luci Swindoll

y parents were very positive people and encouraged each of us kids to think positively about our lives, our school, our friends, and our relationships within the family. Like all children though, we got discouraged at times and pouted. I would confess to my father my fear or insecurity, and Dad would say, "Let's discuss it. If anyone else can get up in front of the class and give a speech, then you can too, and maybe even better." So throughout our childhood we were encouraged to look on the bright side—to be positive.

Yet I've come to realize the downside of always thinking positively—in many ways it caused me to deny the negative feelings I sometimes had—especially the more volatile emotions of anger or frustration.

It's taken me time and counseling with a psychologist to understand it is okay to feel bad, to be angry, to be disappointed. These feelings are just as valid as love and happiness. Letting ourselves feel the full range of emotions gives life balance.

And just as it is okay to acknowledge all of my emotions and feelings, it's okay for me to *show* them as well—even in the workplace. I know from experience there are several emotions we are likely to encounter on the job—anger, frustration, fear, jealousy, and disappointment. But as Christian working women, how do we keep our emotional responses in line with our spiritual walk? What are appropriate responses to our emotional reactions at work?

The Best Laid Plans . . .

During my IBM days my boss promised me a promotion if I met a certain sales quota. I broke my back to do so, only to have the promotion denied. My boss's manager had not given him the okay to make such an offer. I was very upset and decided to speak to my boss's manager. To control my emotions, I wrote out what I intended to say, then slept on it. In his office the next day, my voice started to shake as I pleaded my case. He perceived my fears and jumped on them. My "best laid plans" fell apart. I knew if I said something I'd start to cry. I left feeling so powerless. Today, I know I'd react differently. I'm more in control of my emotions and not as intimidated by men as I once was.

—Mary

The first place I look for clues on how to handle my emotions is the Scriptures. For instance, if I get mad at a co-worker, I need to think, How would I want to be treated if she were mad at me? Luke 6:31 comes to mind: "Do to others as you would have them do to you."

Or one verse I've put into practice just recently is Romans 12:17, "Do not repay anyone evil for evil." Let me give you an example: As the public relations representative for Insight for Living, I handled the negative mail we occasionally received.

The offices for Insight recently moved to a new location, and one or two of our supporters wrote in saying, "How could you use the money I sent for the ministry to move into new offices?" They were very upset. Knowing full well that only a very small fraction of their donation was used for operational expenses, I at first was inclined to tell the writers off. Thankfully, I've learned to take a three-step approach that prevents me from giving in to my emotions and keeps me in line with God's commands.

First, I put myself in the other person's shoes. In the case of these letter writers, they weren't aware that much of the funding for the new offices came from designated giving, rather than their donations. Knowing their complaints were based on partial information helped take the edge off my anger.

Second, I had to remember whatever I told them probably wouldn't be what they wanted to hear. They'd like me to say, "Oops, you're right, we're wrong." And finally, whatever I told them, the third step was to respond in a kind, sensitive way to let them know I understood their point of view.

Sometimes it helps to sleep on a response. Many times if I get a letter like this and respond right away, I'll wait twenty-four hours then re-read my answer. Nine times out of ten, I'll change my response and couch it in softer words.

Tone It Down
While it might seem contrary to our nature, women need to be a little less open about their feelings. When we walk through the office door, we need to check whatever is bothering us. The same can be said about sharing the good things in our life. A co-worker who is having a rotten day may not appreciate Miss Enthusiasm. We've got to temper how we share our emotions and realize it might be more appropriate to deal with them at another time or place.

—Judith

Of course, matching our emotional response to biblical mandates is ideal, but it takes a great deal of spiritual maturity to put this into practice. When our emotions are near the surface, it's not always easy to recall Scripture to control how we respond.

So what other guidelines can we follow?

———◦◦◦———

While it is at times difficult to know exactly what emotional response is most appropriate in the office, a guiding principle that has worked for me is to be honest with myself and anyone else involved in the situation. For instance, if someone is criticizing you in a way that cuts to the core, go ahead and say, "I want you to know that what you're telling me is making me very upset. Perhaps we might be better off talking about this at another time."

Such an open, honest approach can defuse the situation

and help you regain control. Granted, to respond like this to an emotionally heated situation takes a great deal of self-awareness and composure. It takes what I call a "quiet confrontation," which has more often than not been hard for me. But with this approach you preserve your integrity without jeopardizing your work image. This is an area where psychotherapy has been very helpful. I'm learning it's much better to express how I feel than deny those feelings or search for a place inside myself to hide.

It's tempting to counterattack when your emotions are directing your actions. The reason is simple—it's because we're acting in the flesh. And when we operate in the flesh, it never brings glory to God. The flesh and the spirit are two entirely different things. When we're hurt, we want to lash back. Instead, we need to take what the other person is saying and look for the truth in it. There may be something in what we've been told that could help us grow.

If you find yourself responding emotionally to a comment or situation, it helps to look at how you received the information that is upsetting you. I've contended all my life that the worst news in the world can be told if you know how to tell it.

Unfortunately, there are poor communicators as managers and poor leaders who easily hurt people with a lack of tact. When this is the case, it helps to separate the information that has upset or disappointed us from the behavior of the person who delivered the news.

Say you've worked long and hard on a project. But as it turns out, your supervisor only chooses to use a fraction of the information you've provided. Naturally, most of us would be disappointed. But consider two ways your supervisor could convey her thanks for your work to soften your disappointment. The first, "You really missed the boat on this project." Or the second, "I sure appreciate the work you did on this particular project. Unfortunately, we're not going to be able to use everything, but I wanted you to know how grateful I am for your input and your expertise. Let me discuss with you the things we plan to leave out."

Who wouldn't feel their disappointment turn into anger with the first response? So it pays to step back and determine the source of your anger.

A woman I know works in a family-owned business and reports to one of her aunts. For the most part, their relationship goes smoothly. But on occasion this woman admits, "My aunt will do something that gets me upset and I'll think, I never would have done it what way." Over time, however, this woman has learned to step back and ask herself, Is it something in me that's triggering this emotional response, or is it really my aunt's behavior?

Surprisingly, this woman discovered it's not her aunt's behavior that grates on her nerves. Rather, it's basically that her aunt's responses are very similar to her mother's responses—ones that frustrated her while growing up.

Once she came to this realization, she understood her emotional response better and could address the issue that she had been called on rather than respond to her aunt's personality.

———✦———

Other factors that play into how and when emotions are displayed at work include a person's temperament, age, and spiritual maturity.

When we're younger we don't stop and think as often as we should. Instead, we act on impulse. We're more inclined to say things we wish we hadn't. We may be right on the issue, but is it wise to speak out on it? That's the real question.

As we get older, we begin to think, What will be the ramifications of this action? Can I peacefully work with my co-workers or supervisor once I let them know what I think?

Part of wisdom comes from knowing our Bible and seeing its truths put into practice and proven in the workplace. The Bible becomes more than just black words on white paper—it becomes a touchstone. I can now look up certain verses and say, "Yes, this approach works. I've seen it work for me. It is the best."

When I was employed at Mobil, a friend of mine was furious with her boss—he had been continually belittling her.

She was going to tell him off and then quit, if he didn't fire her first. I knew she was a believer, though she wasn't a very active Christian. So when she came to me with news of her intentions, I felt free to interject some biblical principles into our discussion.

I remember telling her, "Let's look at this a little more carefully before you march in there and give your boss a piece of your mind. In the past, you've told me every time you got mad on the job and felt you were being treated unfairly, that you would quit, right? Why don't you apply what the Lord has to say in Hebrews 10:30, 'Vengeance is mine, I will repay' (RSV). Let the Lord take care of the unfair treatment from your boss."

My friend decided to turn the problem over to the Lord and then wait to see what he would do. In time, another employee became enraged at this boss and told him off. The boss was so disgruntled that he eventually quit. My friend was vindicated, and she never had to open her mouth in self-defense. To my knowledge she is still with Mobil. It's the longest job she has ever held because she waited for the Lord to work rather than acting upon her feelings at the moment.

Reaching the Boiling Point

While patience was the key to my friend resolving her work situation, sometimes our anger can't be put on hold. Just as Jesus was justified in reacting with anger when he saw the moneychangers in the temple, so too, there is a place for "righteous indignation" in the workplace. We may not overturn tables, but there may come a time when it's right to stand up for our beliefs at work. The key is maintaining our professionalism while displaying righteous anger. Remember, you're a lady, not a top sergeant!

For instance, we all have those moments when we are justifiably mad at our bosses. But whether or not my anger is justified, I try to get to the root of why I feel the way I do before I act on my emotions. It's a good idea to write down the reasons for your anger. Live with that piece of paper for a few hours or a day, maybe even overnight. Once your reasons for feeling angry are clear, develop in your mind a plan for discussing what is making you upset.

Now, as I confessed earlier, I am not a confronter. To me confronting a person is almost as hard as losing weight. (Of course, *nothing* is more difficult than losing weight!) I tend to think, What if they don't like me for what I'm about to say? I would do almost anything to keep the peace. I know this isn't good, but it's me and it's an area of fear I'm trying to overcome.

So the first thing I try to do is create an atmosphere where the person I'm confronting does not feel denigrated as a person. But the real key is keeping the discussion to the behavior that has caused the upset—not attacking the person. Distinguishing between the two isn't always easy, but it's essential if we hope to confront out of love.

When I have been courageous enough to confront another person, I've always been glad afterward. These situations, though painful, have forced me to stretch beyond my comfort zone. In fact, looking back, I have grown the most as a person through the confrontations I've had.

Turn On the Faucet

Confrontations can elicit a host of emotions, and often they bring on tears. When most women consider the appropriateness of displaying emotions at work, the question of whether or not it's okay to cry ranks at the top. Is it all right? Or is it manipulation?

While it can be very difficult not to cry when you get chewed out for something, I believe it can be inappropriate to cry at work, especially in the presence of a supervisor. It's not that tears make us any less of a person. But rather, crying can reflect a lack of professionalism. A true professional does not personalize everything that happens during the work day. If we do then we're more susceptible to tears.

If you feel as though you're on the verge of crying at work, try saying, "You'll have to excuse me. I don't think I can handle this right now." Then head for the restroom or the privacy of your office and shed your tears there. I've found I am better able to respond to the situation when I've regained my composure. I think it speaks well for the inner qualities of a person when you can do this, and it speaks well of your professionalism.

Although I think it's wise to keep crying to a minimum at the office, we all need to give ourselves a little slack. Realize that some days are better than others. I know that on a particular day someone can tear into me and it might make me fall to pieces. Another day I might say, "So what," to the exact same comments.

Seeing Green

It's not uncommon at some point in a career to be passed over for a promotion or a perk you think you deserve. It's happened to me. A woman was hired to replace a co-worker in my area. One day I was rummaging through the files and quite accidentally discovered that my new co-worker had received a very substantial raise before I did—although I had more seniority and experience. I was hurt and disappointed.

I became distant toward her and finally she confronted me on my behavior. I admitted that I had found out about her salary and couldn't understand why this had happened. "I don't think it's fair," I said. And to my surprise, she answered, "I don't think it's fair either."

She explained the situation. Apparently the salary needed to be upgraded for this particular position and the company did that when they hired her. Soon I would receive a raise, too, and the situation would be a little more equitable.

After this I learned that until all the facts are in, appearances can be deceiving. I was wasting my energy on emotions that had no basis. Now what I try to do and what I recommend to others is to sit down, look within, and say, Look at what you do have. Count your blessings. You've got a great job. You work with great people. And, besides, you may not know the whole story.

For instance, a woman saw her co-worker seemingly take

on new and more exciting responsibilities. She took it very personally and a sense of resentment grew inside her. She really wanted to stomp into her boss's office and say, "I'm not being treated fairly." But she knew that wouldn't accomplish much, if anything. So instead she spent some time praying for God's direction in how she should resolve her feelings of resentment. The answer was to look at her job description and approach her boss with the following comment. "At my last review I said I was 'fairly happy' with my duties and responsibilities. Well, I'd like to know what we can do to move that to a 'very happy' with my job?" Her boss wasn't put on the defensive and they worked out a mutually satisfying agreement. And in the context of the discussion, the woman was able to tell her supervisor—without sounding like a pouting child—that she would really like to do some of the things she saw her co-worker doing.

I Don't Think I Can Do It

One emotion we don't always want to acknowledge in the workplace, though most likely we have experienced it, is fear or feelings of insecurity. Like tears, fear is something that's good to recognize but is best dealt with privately.

We cannot ignore it. We can't act like we're not afraid when we are. It helps to search the Scriptures and take God at his Word when we're in situations that cause us anxiety. I've often called upon Deuteronomy 31:6, "Be strong and courageous. Do not be afraid or terrified because of them, for the LORD your God goes with you; he will never leave you nor forsake you."

We all have times when we wonder if we'll make a deadline, if a presentation will go well, or we feel overwhelmed with responsibilities we don't seem qualified to handle. To keep fear from getting a grip on you, try talking about your feelings with someone close to you. If you can admit your fear, then a friend can help you probe into your feelings more deeply.

I have a friend in Phoenix who is very gifted in television. She had an excellent opportunity to move from one major TV affiliate to another. She called me one night and said, "Luci, I just don't know if I should do it. I feel really insecure about this new offer, yet I also have the feeling I shouldn't pass up this opportunity."

We talked a long time about her successes at her current job and the new challenges that were on the horizon should she decide to change networks. We brainstormed and prayed together over the phone and she hung up feeling more encouraged with her fears alleviated. Our conversation gave her an opportunity to see her situation from another person's perspective—someone who believed in her.

There are a lot of unknowns out there. We think, But what if this happens? What if that happens? What if I fail? Instead, we need to remember, Christ is with us. He has brought us this far. He's not going to give us any more than we can bear.

⎯⎯◈⎯⎯

Many of us spend the majority of our lives in the workplace. It's unrealistic to think we can keep all of our emotions in check every day from nine to five, only letting them show when we're away from the office. If we have to hold back who we are and what we feel simply because we are in a work environment, we end up restricting our God-given gifts. Women, with our unique emotional makeup, bring an invaluable softness and kindness to the workplace. I'm grateful for it and you should be too. The key to expressing emotions at work is keeping them balanced and following God's directives on handling ourselves.

Body Language
Holly G. Miller

Just as reading body language helps us understand other people, "speaking" it helps us to be understood. When our spoken and unspoken communications are in sync, the silent language underscores the spoken language and cranks up the volume of the words. Our message comes through loud and clear.

To help you communicate your message and your emotions more effectively, experts offer these tips:

Hands Down. Try using firm, tight motions rather than sweeping expansive ones when you want to emphasize key points. Men's clipped arm and hand movements are read as being quietly confident, whereas women's large, dramatic gestures sometimes suggest an absence of control.

At Ease. Women often don't use their personal space effectively. We cross our legs tightly, wrap our arms around ourselves, and try to occupy as little room as possible. The message is, "If I make myself small enough, maybe no one will notice me." Particularly in a one-on-one discussion, the person we are talking with will interpret our body language and follow the example we set. If we look comfortable, so will others around us.

Lower Your Voice. Women are blessed with voices that can express a great deal of emotion. But when we become nervous or angry, our voices often climb to a shrill pitch. Practice lowering your voice by finding your normal speaking tone on a piano. Gradually, half step by half step, drop your pitch and read a paragraph out loud at that level. Tape-record your voice to determine if you sound natural, calm, and pleasant.

Wear Cool Colors. If you want to send a message of authority to a boisterous audience (a teenage Sunday school class, for example), wear a dark color. Suits are no longer mandatory dress for professional women. Still, a tailored look prevails, and navy blue or black works best. Balance your "cool" impression with a warm smile.

Hold the Giorgio. According to an unspoken rule, if you are within someone's perfume or after-shave range, you're too close unless you know the person well. Beware of splashing on too much cologne; you may extend your "territory" and make yourself unapproachable to those around you.

Say Cheese. When you answer the telephone, be aware of how you look. Sit up straight, take a deep breath before picking up the receiver, and smile as you say Hello. Although the caller can't see you, she will hear your positive body language as it comes through in your voice.

List When You Listen. When someone is confiding in you, show your interest by leaning slightly forward (the word *listening* comes from "to list" which means to tilt). Encourage your friend by nodding your head as if to confirm that you understand. Occasionally rephrase what she has said to let her know you are following her message. Maintain eye contact but don't stare at her. Know that when she breaks eye contact and looks away, she is handing the conversation to you. It's time for you to respond.

Look Serene as a Swan. If you know you are going to be in a tense situation, position yourself behind a desk where your toes can tap and your fingers can fidget unseen. With less body to manage, you can minimize the telltale signs of nervousness. You will resemble the swan who serenely glides across the water. From the shore, no one can detect her feet paddling feverishly under the surface.

Pause a Moment. The same advice you give your children before they cross a busy street also can help you avoid accidents—communication collisions. Before speaking, take time to pause, look for clues in the other person's face and mannerisms, and listen to what she says and how she says it. Adjust your response to suit the situation.

From Today's Christian Woman
(September/October 1991)

Make It Happen

1. Have a game plan ready for handling situations that are emotionally difficult. For instance, if you're angry, know that you'll go to your office and write yourself a letter about how you feel or you'll read a Bible verse such as Proverbs 29:11, "A fool gives full vent to his anger, but a wise man keeps himself under control." If you cry easily, know where you can go to regain composure without others asking probing questions.

2. Learn to be honest with your emotions. It can be draining to wear a mask to work day in and day out. Find a friend who asks good questions and draws out how you truly feel about situations at work.

3. If you feel as though you're not in control of your emotions, do this quick check: Have you been taking care of yourself properly—exercising, eating right, finding time for things you enjoy? Have you been reading your Bible regularly and sharing

with the Lord your struggles and joys? Have you been keeping up on those friendships that offer you support and perspective? All these areas are key to keeping emotionally healthy.

Chapter 14

HOW CAN I SET REALISTIC CAREER GOALS?
Luci Swindoll

hen I started out with Mobil I never thought, "Someday I'm going to be in management." Initially, I was hired as a junior draftsman fresh out of college. I planned to stay with Mobil for a year, then return to school and acquire my master's degree in art.

But after a year, I was having so much fun I decided to stay another year. Then another. And another. Eventually, I moved from draftsman to technical illustrator, all the time thinking, I like it here. I don't want to leave yet.

Being the type who loves to learn, I soon wanted to explore other job opportunities at Mobil. Bit by bit, through the years, doors opened; and as new opportunities presented themselves, I thought, I'll give it a try.

Finally, when my boss announced his impending retirement, I made known my desire to be considered for his job—a managerial position that had never before been held by a woman. He also informed me that I was being considered.

In the two years before his retirement, I took every opportunity to learn about his work. I asked to join him at meetings, to attend job shows, to represent him at various functions, to prepare certain reports. I wanted to be as qualified as possible when Mobil selected candidates to replace my boss.

Look Before You Leap

I once accepted a job only to find it a total mismatch. I felt guilty about disliking the job and wondered, What's wrong with me? After all, the company had pursued me. I was flattered and figured, If they came to me it must be the right job. Although I didn't want to admit it at first, I hadn't thoroughly investigated the job and jumped too soon. It was not nearly as exciting as I expected, and I left after one year.

—Mary

While there was a lot I didn't know about the position, I was eager to learn. In my heart, I knew I would make a good manager and be able to lead people. A part of me was afraid of the unknown, but the other part of me wanted the responsibility. Soon after my boss retired, I did find myself in his shoes. I ended up in management even though that was not my intent when I was hired so many years before.

To what degree do we need to plan our careers? To what degree do we just let them happen? The answer is a little of both.

Keep Your Eyes Open

If you want to keep your career challenging and growing, stay prepared. Keep your eyes open for opportunities much like I did at Mobil. Beyond that, learn to speak up when those opportunities arise. I know a lot of people who were in the right place at the right time, but never spoke up.

When I attended management school, I confessed that I had at times found it hard to make my desires known. I remember saying to one teacher, "I don't know if I should be that assertive on the job." Her response was, "Yes, you should. There's nothing wrong with saying, 'May I have an opportunity?' " Once I started thinking like this, it really opened doors for me. Don't be afraid to step out and take on a new responsibility. If you want to move ahead in your career, you've got to say, "May I have a chance at this?" Or, "How would you feel if I sit in your place?" If we don't speak out, management quite often thinks, Since she hasn't demonstrated any interest, I assume she's not interested.

At times our interest isn't even expressed in words but in actions. If you're always at work on time, dependable, and eager to learn, believe me that gets noticed. Management often notes, She did a great job on that. She's top notch. She hasn't said much, but let's watch her.

If you want to move up within a company, experience has shown me it's not necessary to claw and scratch your way ahead. Rather, it's doing well at what you are asked to do, then having the confidence to move along with the assurance the Lord is the one who is opening the doors.

Seeing beyond the Present

Stretch a Little

Careers today are ever changing. Gone are the days you trained for one profession and stuck with it all your life. It's my hope more women will embrace the opportunity to learn something new—to change direction and look at the benefits of having multiple careers. Learning something new builds self-confidence and also allows us to better understand ourselves and the world around us.

—Judith

Although I wasn't convinced of this twenty years ago, I am today—the career path you are on today need not be something that must continue forever. What you're doing today is most likely relative to a certain time period in your life. Unfortunately, some people tend to think in absolutes—I'm locked in this job forever. It's a dead-end street. In reality, it probably isn't. It's how you view the situation that makes it a dead-end street.

We've all been in situations where it's hard to see beyond the present. I recall times when I've been so physically ill that I didn't have the energy to walk to the kitchen and make a cup of tea. In the middle of the illness, I was sure I'd never get well again. My only focus was on the present. On the sickness. On the confinement.

We can fall into this type of thinking in work situations as well. We might think we'll never get the skills to move up or change jobs. But we need to have the maturity to realize we will not always be sick or stuck in a job we feel is going nowhere. And once we can distinguish between the absolute and the relative,

we free our minds to plan for the next step—the very step that
will move us up and out.

———

But even if we have those "pit stops" in our careers, it's
important to realize we're learning more about ourselves and life
in the process. In my book *After You Dress for Success* (Word), I wrote
about creating a "lifeline" for myself.

I encourage every working woman to do the same. Draw a
line across the page representing your "average" life from birth to
your present age. Then, put all the positive, significant events or
circumstances that have happened in your life above the line.
Next, indicate the difficult, negative events below that line, at the
approximate age they occurred. Thankfully, much of my life has
been positive—I had wonderful parents, great siblings, a wonderful education. But I had two times that were very low—two
occasions that fell very far below average. The first was fighting
for my own autonomy, to be myself and not a prefabrication of
my mother's desires for me. It had to do with all the pain of
individuating in my twenties. The other was in my forties when
I moved to the West Coast from Texas. I thought, You've cut the
umbilical cord. You can never go back. I'm so sorry I came out
here. This is too hard! I had to start over with new friends, a new
career, new surroundings. A very difficult period!

But when I look back on my life now, the deepest learning
about myself and life came from those two low points that were
so difficult for me to bear. When you hit rock bottom ask yourself, What did that mean to me? What was of value in that?
Then take what you've learned and apply it to the goals you
have for your career. It will make your goals and expectations
more realistic.

As M. Scott Peck says in the opening line of his book *The
Road Less Traveled* (Touchstone), "Life is difficult." But, when we
learn to look at all that happens to us and say, "There is something in this for me," growth will occur. Believe me, the Lord
wouldn't put you where you are unless you needed to learn
something about yourself and what career is best for you.

Just as a certain career path isn't set in stone, neither should we feel our education or training for a job should keep us on only one path. A classroom education is only a tool and when we look at it as such, it opens all kinds of doors. It's not a be-all and end-all—it's the beginning. It's a way of disciplining our thinking, it's a way of defining some basic interests. Education is a never-ending process, and the same is true in setting career goals.

I've retired once, only to start another career. And now that I've retired again, I have a new set of goals for my life. Every change brings fresh ways of looking at things.

Trust the Lord for His Direction

As we carve out our career and set certain goals, it's vital we have a sense of trust in the Lord's direction for our lives. Yet how do we build that trusting relationship? For me it came in a surprising way—through tithing. Now I know this seems to have very little to do with deciding to take a job promotion or not, but let me explain.

Two-and-a-half years ago, I decided I would tithe. For years I had tithed on and off, but never consistently nor at a level that made it seem like a true sacrifice. But I made it a goal that out of my gross pay I'd tithe 12 to 15 percent no matter what! I didn't know how I'd do it but I said, "Lord, you said if we do what you command, you will honor it. Now finally, after all these years, I'm going to take you at your Word and see what happens."

Hardly a month has gone by that I have not thought at some point, I'm going to run out of money this month. I'm not going to be able to pay the rent. Yet each time I've kept my promise, and the Lord has met my needs. It might be the eleventh hour, but he has been utterly trustworthy. And it's been amazing and exciting to watch him work.

My "experiment" has proven to me two important truths.

First, I've learned I can completely take God at his Word. Money is something near and dear to all of us, and if we can build our trust in the Lord on that level, think how faithful he will be when it comes to questions about career choices—or anything else.

Second, tithing has helped me have the courage to discipline myself in many other areas of my life. It has helped me set goals and *reach* those goals.

Once we learn to trust the Lord's promises, we will see his amazing faithfulness. For me, seeing that he does what he says gives me respect for who he is as my Father. It also gives me a tremendous peace. I know he's not going to leave me without comfort or without direction. Like I said, the effect of learning to trust the Lord in one area flows over into all areas of our lives—especially our careers.

From Better to Best

I cannot say too much about prayer—it's absolutely vital as we make decisions about our careers. We need to continually ask the Lord for his guidance, his direction. It's hard to separate the good from the better and the better from the best.

We usually have little difficulty separating the good from the bad. The challenge comes when we ask, "Which is best for me, Lord? I'm happy where I am, but a door is open over there. Should I go through it?" Don't say yes too fast, but don't say no either. Take advantage of waiting and thinking and praying *now*. I've known people who were ready but were too scared to do anything. Or others who were not afraid to move ahead yet weren't ready. Think about it. Pray about it. As it is written in Matthew 10:16, "Be as shrewd as snakes and as innocent as doves."

Often I've discovered we don't know why we've been put on a particular career path, but there's something about it that feels right. I believe we have natural inclinations toward certain fields, and if we're trained in those areas, we'll move toward them. I put a great deal of confidence in a gut-level assurance that a move is right for me. And I believe the reason it's trust-worthy is in part because the Spirit resides in me and helps me recognize the right path to take.

What Do You Want?

When I was twelve years old I knew I wanted a career. I wanted to make money. I wanted to be a business woman. My plans didn't include marriage or a family. Instead, I wanted to write, work, travel abroad, and meet interesting people. As I look back, I've done what I set out to do. I can look at my life and say, "I've had a wonderful life. I've done all these things that I wanted to do." At times, I occasionally think, I'm sorry I didn't marry and have a family. But I know in all honesty that wasn't a priority and I have no regrets.

As you set your career goals, it boils down to figuring out what you really want; look for what expresses the ultimate *you*. Is what I'm doing worth the investment required? After all, if you value your career, you're going to invest in it—be it time, energy, or money. Is it worth the time? Is it worth the energy? Is it worth the money? If the answer is no to any of these questions, it's time to rethink where you are.

Like I did at Mobil, you need to study the avenues of possible career paths. Observe those who are above you. Look at the sacrifices they have made and ask yourself if you'd be willing to do the same. It even pays to read as much about a field as you can get your hands on.

If you're interested in a certain career path, ask yourself a series of "what ifs." What if I go this route instead of some other route? What if, over time, my chosen career loses its appeal? What if the career I want to choose is outside my natural bent?

Realize, too, that what you want as a career may change with time. And as basic as this sounds, be sure your career goals are achievable. If you want to be a Metropolitan Opera star, you've got to be able to sing. But if you do have a realistic plan, be willing to take a few risks to meet your goal.

───⋘⊙⋙───

I've written out goals all my life—including what I want out of my career. For me it's quite natural since I tend to be very goal-oriented and seldom operate out of my hip pocket. Putting goals in writing is not abandoning faith in God. In fact, it helps us achieve things we might not otherwise attempt.

A few years ago I mapped out on paper when I would like to retire (this was my *first* retirement, from Mobil) , how many books I wanted to have written by then, what I wanted to do after retirement, how much money I wanted to be making—the works.

And do you know what? Every single thing that I put down I did—only one year earlier than I had projected! The delineation of goals and writing them down started me doing what I knew in my mind I wanted to accomplish—and that's the importance of writing down goals. It might be scary at first, but I can tell you from experience it absolutely works. It offers you a chance to deal with the unknown before you get there. To a certain degree, it gives you a chance to know your life in advance—it makes you think ahead and get things in the order of their importance. Of course, it doesn't mean everything is going to work out the way we planned—but it does give us a hope and design for things to work out for the best.

Take, for instance, the desire to be an entrepreneur—to open your own business—at some time in the future. To make it happen tomorrow, you must set some things in motion today. Short-range and long-range goals are the key. It also pays to divide your goals into manageable parts. You're less likely to procrastinate, and you'll be in a better position to jump at an opportunity when the iron is hot.

───⋘⊙⋙───

At some point, many Christians consider a career in formal ministry. In some respects, I hate the word ministry—it separates us from who we are in Christ. No matter where we work or what we do, if Christ is in us that is where our ministry lies. You can minister while sweeping the floor, while serving breakfast to your family, or while checking groceries at the local supermarket. Remember, your ministry is who you are, not what you do.

If we wait for a formal ministry opportunity to come around, chances are the ministry we can and should be doing will never get done. Instead, we need to live every day in the present and do the best we can where we are. Look at where God has placed you and declare that your ministry.

A Crooked Career Path

When I was younger I was very idealistic. I thought Utopia was over every hill. But, as always, life did not live up to my expectations. And so it can be with our careers.

You think your career will be one way, only to find it's not at all like you envisioned. If you're frustrated with the current direction of your career, remember God is still at work. First, he is working to bring those who don't know him to a knowledge of himself. And second, he is working to bring those who know him into a place of maturity—and sometimes that is done through the ups and downs of a career.

As we move through life, our careers knock the rough edges off us—we are changed and molded in the process. Whether we like it or not, we learn the hard way and are more cautious the next time our steps are directed down one career path or another.

No one has all the answers, and planning a career is by no means an exact science. I often look at my brother Chuck and think, "He's a theologian. He's been in public ministry thirty years. There's not a day in his life he doesn't study the Bible. He's bound to know the answer to such and such."

So I ask him something like, "Why do bad things happen to good people?"

And he'll say, "I don't know."

"You've got to know," I'll say. "You're the theologian."

We learn what is right for us by doing. By making mistakes. By changing our course when we know it's not the best for us.

As we map out our careers, I like to recall the words of George Washington Carver: "How far you go in life depends on your being tender with the young, compassionate with the aged, sympathetic of the striving, and tolerant of the weak and the strong because someday in life you will have been all of these."

What a guideline to follow!

Make It Happen

1. Read Psalm 127:1-2 and relate it to how you should go about setting career goals. Who should be involved in whatever your job might be? Is what you're doing or hoping to do glorifying God? Also read 1 Peter 2:11-17 on the parameters a Christian should use in determining her life's work.

2. Look back over your career(s). What are some of the best insights you've gained about yourself, about a career, about people? What are some of the most difficult lessons you've learned? Remember, those lessons that are particularly difficult to accept may not surface for months. Give yourself time to process situations. But when you do come to an insight, take a moment to make a mental note or write it down in your journal.

3. Write out a job description of your dream career. Is it reasonable? Does it best utilize the unique gifts God has given you? Show it to a friend. Does she think it agrees with what you are capable of doing? Bring your ideal job description before the Lord. Ask him in his unlimited creativity to help it become a reality.

Chapter 15

IF A POOR DECISION ON MY PART DAMAGES MY CHRISTIAN WITNESS, HOW CAN I REBUILD IT?
Mary Whelchel

n the last company I worked at before I started the radio ministry, I had several opportunities to witness to co-workers. One man, a fellow manager, was a believer but had never had good Christian teaching. He was like a sponge—wanting to learn more and more about what it meant to be a Christian. Seldom did a day go by when we didn't talk about the Lord. Soon he was reading his Bible and praying daily—something he had never done before.

My co-worker wanted a closeness to the Lord like he saw in me, and he was certainly making great strides. I was excited to see how God was using me in his life, too.

Then it happened. A meeting I don't think I'll ever forget. The president of the company, who was an extremely difficult man, called several managers into his office, including this co-worker and me. The president started making derogatory remarks about several staff members I managed. I could feel my temper flaring up. Then he presented a policy he wanted to implement among the staff that I thought was terribly unfair. That was the final straw. I blew up at him! And as I defended my staff and my position on the policy, I said a lot of things I shouldn't have. Soon the president and I were in the middle of a yelling match. The other managers present tried to calm us down and eventually they succeeded.

To this day, I know I was right on the issues at hand. But I should have held my tongue and come back at another time when I was in better control of myself. No matter how right I was, my response to the president was anything but Christian.

Keep the Good Moments Current

We will have failures in the work-place. And often, when we let ourselves down, we stay tuned to them rather than focusing on the good aspects of our work. We continue to beat ourselves up and discount all the positive things we've done. We need to break out of this myopic thinking and instead, as we assess those failures, remember and take credit for our accomplishments.

—Judith

I walked out of that meet-ing, went to my car, and drove home. All I could think was, This is it—I've blown my witness. I've made a total fool of myself in front of a person I've been trying to disciple and another man who doesn't even know the Lord.

At home that night I kept thinking, I can't go back in that office. I was sure I had ruined it for the Lord, and I would never recover from this mistake.

Of course, I knew I had to go back. So in my time with the Lord the next morning, I asked for his guidance. The Lord said to me, "Go back in and tell your friend you blew it. But let him know you've asked for forgiveness and I've forgiven you." My dread of returning to the office was slowly replaced with calm-ness and assurance.

I could tell my co-worker was a little uncomfortable when I got to the office. He didn't know what to say, so I broke the ice and said, "I'm so sorry I blew it in front of you and the others yesterday. There was no excuse for my behavior; I was out of control."

Then I told him how apprehensive I was about returning to the office because I knew I had damaged my testimony. Yet despite my actions, I knew that God had forgiven me and offered me a clean slate. I was starting over this morning, and I hoped he would be able to forgive me.

His response took me completely by surprise. Tears started to run down his cheeks. For some time, he had been struggling with failure and understanding God's forgiveness. And not until that moment did he really understand what God's forgiveness meant. My "damaged witness" turned out to be a great spiritual lesson for this Christian co-worker.

This experience proved to me that I can expect our wonderful, creative God to take those times I blow it *and*, if I handle them correctly, use my failure for his gain. Sometimes, as I learned in this situation, letting our co-workers see we aren't perfect can be a blessing in disguise. Everyone fails at some time—

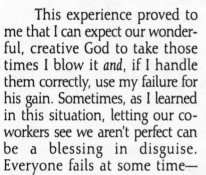

Life Goes On

We tend to be too critical of ourselves. We think, I'm no good or otherwise I wouldn't have done this. But our mistakes only remind us of our humanity and the Lord's promise that he will be our strength in our weakness. In my twenties, if I blew something at work I would be very upset. Now, with more years of living, I know whatever my mistake, life goes on. God is sovereign and I will be forgiven.

—*Luci*

Christians and non-Christians alike. And our co-workers who don't know the Lord know they fail but they don't know what to do about it. They might pretend the failure didn't happen or cover it up. But a sense of guilt shadows them. They have no place to turn to get rid of that guilt. But then they see us— Christians who make mistakes—coming back to the office the next day saying, "I'm forgiven. I'm starting fresh." They see in us that the damage wasn't beyond repair and, more importantly, what a difference the Lord makes in our lives.

When we do fail in our witness, especially if we've been very vocal about our faith, our first thought is, *I've got to get out of here.*

Of course, this is a normal reaction. But rarely does God let us run away. God is not involved in cover-ups. I believe he exposes us for our own good. He wants us to deal with the tough spots.

If your behavior falls short of Christian standards, you need to go back and apologize. Admit you shouldn't have said what you did or acted the way you did—that it was wrong. Let your co-workers know, like I did, that God has forgiven you and you hope they can, too.

Just this past year I had to face the consequences of a broken commitment to a client. I'd like to think I'm beyond such obvious pitfalls, but this incident was a needed reminder that I will always be vulnerable to human failure and sin.

I had made the commitment in haste, knowing I shouldn't have said yes in the first place. I didn't think any harm would come from it, so I forgot about it. However, God didn't. A few weeks later my client learned what I had done and called to confront me. My first inclination was to rationalize, but thankfully the Spirit of God within me reminded me I was wrong, and I admitted it.

I then had to call a woman involved in the situation to apologize and ask her forgiveness. This was particularly difficult because I had witnessed to her and knew she placed a lot of trust in me. I didn't want to make the phone call, but I did as quickly as possible. She expressed her disappointment and thanked me for being up front. We then had a chance to discuss how God is good and faithful even when his children are not.

Despite my terrible failure, God managed to salvage the situation and some good came from it. I wish it had never happened—it didn't do my testimony any good, and the name of Christ would have been more honored had I done the right thing at the beginning—but I encourage you to realize failure is not the end. It's not something to take lightly, but neither is it a reason to be despondent.

Should I Always Ask for Forgiveness?

While forgiveness is a key component to restoring relationships with our co-workers, is an apology always in order? After that meeting between the company president and the managers, I did ask for my co-worker's forgiveness. But I didn't go in and apologize to the president. Why?

For one, the president would have discounted my apology— it would have meant nothing to him. And, in the course of the meeting, we had settled the matter under discussion. But my most important reason for not going back to his office is that I did not feel a leading from God.

As you figure out how to handle a situation in which you've damaged your witness, trust that the Lord will make his direction clear to you.

If we're willing to apologize to a co-worker and wonder if that is the step to take, have confidence the Lord will lead you to do so. There are times we need to go back, other times we don't. And even though I didn't personally apologize to the president, my actions toward others spoke for me.

On the last day I worked for this man he called me into his office. For the first time in four years, he was at a loss for words. Normally he's in control of every situation. He hedged a bit and finally said, "I don't know what to say except I wish I could be as good as you are." He saw me as good—even though I had blown it that one time and many others. Yet he had watched how I worked—he had seen something different in how I handled myself and others.

Do Others Keep a Score Card?

Of course, when we do injure our witness we wonder, What will others think? While I don't think we should live our lives concerned about how others perceive us, as Christians we should try to lead lives that are circumspect. We should try to avoid the appearance of evil and not to bring disgrace to Jesus Christ.

As my relationship with Jesus matures, I've found that I am less controlled by what others think of me. The more I focus on pleasing the Lord, the less time I spend worrying about what others think. And, of course, the more I please Jesus the more people I'm bound to make happy, though I realize I will never be able to please everyone, no matter how solid my record as a Christian.

If you think a co-worker is keeping a score card on your behavior and talking behind your back, remember, everything in us wants to defend our reputation. But nine times out of ten we should keep our mouths shut.

Do the best you can. If you owe an apology, then apologize; if you don't, then let the matter go. Resist the temptation to be defensive and simply realize you will be criticized. You cannot please everyone all the time, and some people will misunderstand you no matter what you do.

If a co-worker is being extremely critical of you and your behavior, often the root is jealously, or possibly you are a threat to her ambitions.

A woman recently wrote me about a manager she worked for who was terribly insecure. The manager was afraid this woman might be promoted over her; she saw her good job performance as a threat. Within a short time, the manager was manufacturing negative reports about this woman simply to make her look bad.

I felt for this woman—under direct attack merely because she did a good job. Because the negative reports were stemming from her manager, this woman would probably suffer unjustly, until someone higher up caught on. In cases like hers, giving a situation time, although it may be hard, is often the only choice you have.

The other step you can take if you honestly think a co-worker is unhappy with you—that words are being spoken behind your back—is to find an occasion to address your concern directly with that co-worker, especially if it happens to be your supervisor.

Be diplomatic in your approach. Try something like, "I'd like some feedback from you. I'd like to do the best job I can. Where do I need to improve? How can I do my job better?" An employee who takes a proactive approach is much better off than one who sits and worries. By kindly confronting the person from whom you feel ill will, you give them a chance to say, "Yes, everything is fine," or "No, here's what is bothering me." From here the door is open for discussion.

I do wish more Christians would be up front like this—it's certainly better than letting our imaginations run wild and thinking the worst. If you feel there is something in a relationship that isn't right, take the initiative. Go out to lunch with that person. Talk over a cup of coffee. Our goal as Christians at work is to promote harmony, and that can't happen when we let our thoughts drift toward the negative.

Just a final word about thoughts. I'm convinced we really have to watch out for the mental tricks our mind can play on us. I have written a study called "The Freedom of a Captive Mind," which is based on Philippians 4:8, "Finally, brethren, whatever is true, whatever is honorable, whatever is just, whatever is pure, whatever is lovely, whatever is gracious, if there is any excellence, if there is anything worthy of praise, think about these things" (RSV).

As you fall short in your witness, and I'm certain we all will at some point in our careers, what are your thoughts about the situation? Do you know for a fact that your co-workers think less of you? That they will now doubt the sincerity of your faith? It's very easy for us to allow something small to get blown out of proportion in our minds. We can actually be too sensitive, too hard on ourselves, too focused on our behavior. If our enemy Satan can't trip us up by making us unaware or oblivious to our failures, he'll try to handicap us by causing us to be uptight and far too self-conscious.

Get in the habit of true thinking. Is what you are thinking reality-based? If not, don't allow untrue thoughts to remain in your head. Doing so is sin. Besides, untrue thoughts tend to multiply in our minds causing us to become more frustrated and angry over a situation, often without a valid reason.

Realize that within our very reach is all we need to pick up the pieces when we blow it—God's Word, his guidance through the Holy Spirit, and his continual, unending forgiveness. No matter how many times we stumble in our walk with the Lord, God uses us wherever we are and causes good to come out of every situation.

Make It Happen

1. Do you need to apologize or set things straight with your co-workers or manager? Is there an incident in the past that warranted your apology but instead you left the issue unresolved? If so, the sooner you go back and admit your failure and ask for forgiveness, the sooner you'll be free to start with a clean slate and move ahead with the Lord. It's painful, but it's a necessary part of living a truthful life. However, don't go digging things up that aren't there. If you need to apologize, God will make you aware of it in your daily quiet times.

2. As Christians we have two natures—the new nature we received when we accepted Christ and the old nature, which is inclined to sin and selfishness. The one you feed is the one that will be strong. Romans 7 is a good chapter to describe the struggle between our two natures. But Romans 8 tells us we can be victorious. Read these two chapters repeatedly. Understanding the warfare between your two natures is essential in dealing with failure in your life.

3. For those times you do blow it, make yourself talk it out with a trusted friend. Force yourself to keep the situation out in the open—this helps avoid the tendency to suppress those things we find humiliating and embarrassing. If you admit to the mistake immediately, you'll be more likely to correct it and deal with it head on. If admitting openly to your imperfections seems awkward at first, keep at it. Over time, this response will come more naturally. You'll be surprised how much easier it is to travel toward Christian maturity when you aren't carrying excess baggage.

Chapter 16

HOW CAN I ENDURE A JOB I FIND UNBEARABLE BUT CAN'T AFFORD TO QUIT?
Mary Whelchel

The last job I had before I started my radio ministry was not my favorite! I liked neither the content of the job nor the man I worked for. For the first year, it seemed the obvious answer was to escape the situation. I remember thinking, *I've got to get out of here. It can't be right to work here—especially for a boss who is so difficult.*

So I polished up my resume and went on several interviews—certain I would soon be out of this unbearable job. The interviews went well, yet I was never offered a job. Finally, I had an interview to go back to IBM. For IBM to rehire you after you've left is almost unheard of, but the man I interviewed with liked what he saw and was going to hire me. He was preparing the paperwork when suddenly he was promoted to another location with IBM. He didn't have time to finish the hiring process, and the job fell through.

Until that point in my career, I had been able to move any time I wanted. I had great confidence in my abilities and credentials. But when I most wanted to make a change, nothing was coming my way. Soon I realized the closed doors were not accidents. God did not intend for me to leave this job just yet.

Finally, after a year with the job I told the Lord, "Okay. I'll stay here if that's what you want me to do."

Until I was able to say those words I was one miserable woman. I stayed with the job for another two-and-a-half years. In that time, I witnessed the greatest growth in my spiritual life I had ever experienced. I learned what it meant to walk with the Lord—to trust and depend on him in a way I had never had to before.

Get Unstuck

If you're in an intolerable job, get your resume prepared and move on. There is work out there and many techniques to get yourself noticed. So often we end up working in jobs that don't fit us because we've listened to what others think is good for us; we let indecisiveness keep us grounded. I say, "Get moving."

—Judith

You may be in a similar position—boxed into a job that doesn't suit your personality, or is difficult to endure because of tensions between you and your boss or co-workers. Or maybe the job is tedious and unchallenging. Whatever the circumstances, the result is the same—work becomes a chore.

While this might seem like simplistic advice, the first step toward turning an unbearable job into something that brings joy and bears fruit is to accept the situation, like I finally did.

It took me months to come to the point where I said, "Okay, I accept this." You can save yourself a lot of anguish if today you acknowledge the situation and say, "This is where I am. For whatever reason, I can't leave this job right now. I accept this job as from the Lord. Nothing happens to me by accident. God hasn't forgotten me. There's something here for me that I can't see, but I trust him." Believe me, even saying that is one big step in the right direction.

If you choose the opposite route and say, "I hate this job—it's not for me," you'll find each day is worse than the one before it. As soon as I relinquished the situation to the Lord, I had a peace about it. I no longer hated to go to work. Relinquishing the situation to the Lord was not a once-and-be-done-with-it action, however. It was a daily task. While I committed myself to surrender my negative feelings, on any given day I could have easily reversed that commitment. I had to ask the Lord to get me through every day.

Making the Unbearable Bearable

As impossible as it may seem, you need to work at maintaining a positive attitude. I find so many people, Christians and non-Christians alike, dwell on the negative. Yet of all the people in the workplace, Christians should be leaders in possessing a positive outlook—after all, we have the most to be positive about.

Hidden Lessons

Expect some disappointments and difficulties. After all, that's how we grow. I used to think there must be an easier way, some shortcut, but I can attest there isn't. We need to look at those tough spots with the attitude, There is something in this for me. Don't miss it. Often we're so certain there is nothing beneficial for us in a situation when indeed there is a lesson we need to learn.

—Luci

Instead, we often feed continuous negative thoughts into our minds. We sit around and talk about the job and say, "I can't stand my job. I hate my boss." A steady diet of talk like that and soon we've convinced ourselves there is nothing redeeming about our work.

Instead, make your talk positive and encouraging. I gave myself pep talks like, "You know, Lord, this is probably not my first choice as a job, but it is better than being unemployed. I appreciate the fact that I have an income in a time many are unemployed. I know there are others who'd be thrilled to have this job. I know it doesn't use all my talents or abilities but it's better than nothing."

It helps to realize that your current job probably is not the worst job in the world. If you think hard enough, I'm sure you can imagine worse positions to hold. Consider the good that's coming from the job you now hold. A positive attitude leads to a thankful heart. Most likely you receive a regular paycheck, you can meet your bills, and you won't be going hungry. Be thankful that your job enables you to meet the basic needs of life.

Positive thinking is a biblical principle. Just read Philippians 4:8—that passage clearly tells us to think about what is noble, true, right, and lovely. If we fill our minds with positives, there should be little room left for the negatives that can drag us down and zap our energy. Make it your daily prayer to say, "Lord, help me to develop and maintain a positive attitude so that I see the good things."

Likewise, be wise as to whom you associate with on the job. Negativity is infectious. Someone else's pessimistic attitude and words can seep into your mind and cause you to become downcast. We don't want to lower ourselves to their level. Instead, we must put a shield around our minds and, if necessary, physically remove ourselves to protect our minds from the negativity of others.

Take the Creative Twist

When people are dissatisfied with a job, I've noticed they often fail to take a very essential step toward making the situation tolerable: They lose their creativity. Experience has shown me those who become successful first become "president" of their job. They aren't confined by what the job description says.

If you don't like your job description, get creative about what you can do to change it, to enlarge it. Granted, that's not always possible, but it is possible more often than most of us think. Bring into the job something that interests you, that makes you want to come into the office each morning.

An acquaintance of mine told me how she was frustrated with her job because it didn't use all of her skills. So I said, "Then write your own job description. What do you want to do?" Until that point, she had never considered this option. She couldn't see beyond the fact that she disliked her position.

Ask yourself, "What do I want to do that they're not letting me do? What could I do that no one else is doing?" Ask your boss, "Can I do this? I really think this would be beneficial to my job and the company."

No job is 100 percent satisfying. No matter what our job, we'll always have those tasks that are tedious and unfulfilling. But if you begin to think creatively about your work, you may find that there are some unexplored options available to you.

Keeping Motivated

How can you stay motivated to do your best in a job you dislike? It's not easy, but, as I discovered, it is possible. The key is to depend on the Lord daily for the motivation you need. Each day I literally said, "Lord, motivate me today. I can't do it, and I know it's giving up to say, 'I can't.' You said I *can* do all things through you and I'm claiming that promise today. Help me do a good job today just because I'm working for you."

If you take this lesson to heart—depending on the Lord to work through you and motivate you—its benefits will reach far beyond the workplace and your present situation. You'll find you have mastered a skill that will help you get through many difficult challenges throughout life.

But responding like this to those things we don't like to do requires a great deal of personal and spiritual maturity. And even then, it can be hard to push ourselves. I certainly didn't succeed every day to keep a positive attitude and dive into my work. There were some days I struggled to do more than sit at my desk. I remember thinking, This is a bad decision on God's part for me to be here. Yet all signs indicated he was actively choosing to keep me where I was. Looking back I now realize one of the reasons he kept me there was so I would learn to lean on his understanding instead of my own.

Rounding Out Life

Another way to counteract your displeasure with a certain job is to look at your entire life for balance. You spend only part of your day at the job, but what are you doing with your off-hours?

When I was in the job I so disliked, I was fortunate enough to be in the initial stages of developing my radio ministry. I also was starting to do some public speaking and had begun a ministry for working women at my church. Being involved in these activities I loved made it easier to tolerate a job that wasn't very pleasant. Look at your interests and hobbies. What can you do to bring a sense of joy into your life from pursuits other than work?

Putting in Time

At certain points in a career, we must simply put in time. Your current position may be one of those instances. Yet, a lot of people aren't willing to pay their dues. I have people in their twenties and thirties come up to me after a seminar and say, "I want to do what you're doing. How do I get started?"

I say, "First of all, you need a good deal of experience. My years at IBM and other companies have given me the background to be a business trainer." Their enthusiasm fades once they understand I'm not talking about a year or two of experience, but maybe ten to twenty years.

You can't shortchange experience. It takes time to build credibility and knowledge. And every step you're taking today is preparing you for tomorrow. The first ten years of my work experience consisted mainly of secretarial-type work. I moved into a sales position with IBM in my early thirties, and my colleagues were, for the most part, young college graduates. I didn't realize it at the time, but I was leaps and bounds ahead of them for one simple reason—I knew how offices were run and I could use my knowledge to reinforce my sales pitch for office products. When I talked with customers, I could discuss real-life problems and challenges. After all, I had once been in their shoes. The new graduates, on the other hand, had to rely on a memorized sales pitch. Putting in my time paid off.

Paying our dues in a job we dislike can be rewarding, although we might not see the returns immediately. It took me years to see why God wanted me in the position I so disliked before moving into my radio ministry. But now I know it was for my own spiritual growth—the many insights I gained I now share with others. During those three-and-a-half years the Lord taught me the difference between walking alone in my Christian growth and walking with him. He used me as a witness to co-workers I had never considered witnessing to, and finally I learned some business skills that would be vital to successfully starting my own business.

But isn't it always the case? The pieces fall together in the end even though we don't see the wisdom along the way. You have to trust God. It's only through hindsight that you see how he weaves all of the threads together.

Lead by the Dollar

In our society we value people for the amount of money they make. Sadly, this type of thinking has crept into our Christian mindset too. I'll admit, each year as I see my income go down, I start to feel like I have less value. I know these wrong thoughts come from buying into the world's system. Unfortunately, the money trap is a big one. And it's one of the biggest reasons people stay in jobs they hate.

For many of us, the pay may be great from our job, but that's all. The problem with earning a good salary is that we tend to lock ourselves into a standard of living based on the money we make. Then we lose the freedom to leave our job if and when we want to.

If you feel it is time to move to a new position, yet the money issue is holding you back, ask yourself, "Where do I find my security?" If a majority of your decisions are based on money, you cannot be walking by faith.

There may be a time when God says, "I really want you out of here." Your response might be, "But I don't know where I could find a job that pays as much as this one." The economy might be bad, jobs may not be plentiful, but I think there are times when God pushes us out to the edge so we can learn to walk by faith.

A friend of mine with four children returned to the workplace once her kids were in school. She took a job with a poorly managed company, and the result was she worked a lot of overtime and felt tremendous pressure added to her already demanding position as wife, mother, and homemaker. Although the situation was extremely stressful, she stuck it out knowing she would need some experience to be marketable for another position. After a year, though, she decided the pressure was too great. I remember her saying, "This just isn't good for me or my family."

My friend left her job without having another one lined up. She took a step in faith and trusted that the Lord would provide for her family and help her find the right job opportunity. This is another situation where you need "forever eyes." Don't let money be your master. Ask yourself, Is it worth it? Look what I'm doing to myself. Look what I'm doing to my family.

My son-in-law is very bright and talented and loves his job as a producer of a Christian radio program for teens. He could earn more if he chose to leave this job, but he understands a critical truth: more money doesn't necessarily mean more satisfaction.

Recently, he was given a great job appraisal, and I asked him if he had any aspirations to move into management. "I don't know if I want management," he said. "At least not now. I am really happy where I am."

Many people wrongly assume that career success comes from climbing higher and higher within the corporation. We are wise when we understand that job success is measured by how happy we are doing our work. If you like what you do, perhaps it is smarter to stay where you're at, even if a promotion presents itself. Discontentment is often purchased at the price of a higher salary or a prestigious title. We need to have confidence in where God has placed us.

What a Job Can't Do

If you think a job is going to fulfill you completely, you're in for a big disappointment—it can't and it won't. Nothing on earth can fulfill us completely. Until Jesus Christ is the center of your life, you will always feel a void. I've seen plenty of mothers with darling little children and wives with nice husbands who are unfulfilled. And I've seen women in top-notch positions who will tell me privately, "Is this all there is?" We need to realize a career can offer only a certain amount of fulfillment.

Make Jesus the focus of your life. When we do that, we no longer expect something out of our job that it can never offer.

Some Days I Hate This Job!
Holly Green

You've had it with your job. You're overworked, underpaid, and burned out. Take heart! You're not alone. Whatever our occupation, we all have occasions when we're fed up. Before you hand in your resignation letter and rewrite your resume, consider these ideas for coping with work-related frustrations.

Battle Boredom. Is your job tedious? Take on additional duties. Assist someone proficient in a skill you'd like to learn. Work at upgrading your skills to be eligible for more interesting responsibilities.

Set Priorities. If you panic under a heavy workload, organize your time so you do the essential work first and save the less urgent for last. Keep a checklist and mark off tasks completed.

Repair Relationships. Most unhappiness at work stems not from the job itself but from relationship conflicts. Is there a person with whom you don't get along? Then confront the problem head on. It's difficult, but try something like, "I feel things aren't right between us. I'm sorry for anything I did. Can we start over?"

Find a Confidant. Share job frustrations with a mature person outside the work environment. Look for someone who keeps confidences well and offers sympathy but also holds you accountable to work on solutions to your problems.

Expand Your Interests. Remember, work is only one aspect of your life. Don't expect it to meet your every need. Put your energies into a variety of relationships and activities—family, friends, church, classes, clubs, community service.

Watch for Lessons. Keep your eyes open for what the Lord wants to teach you. He can turn bad times into opportunities for growth. If you are being treated badly, for example, use it to learn to treat others well.

Let God Use You. Have you considered that he has put you in your job for a reason? Be his instrument to make a difference where you are. Don't ask for relief; ask to be the one who brings relief to others.

Take Inventory. Just how bad is your situation? Write down the pros and cons of your position. Does one list balance the other? This may help you determine whether you are well-suited to your work, or whether the job really isn't a good fit and it's time to change.

From Today's Christian Woman
(January/February 1991)

Make It Happen

1. Make a list of all the things you are thankful for at your current place of employment. It may even be trivial things—like free coffee, a nice chair, one person who is friendly and positive. Then be thankful! Ask the Lord to open your eyes to the "haves" in your job rather than the "have-nots."

2. Listen to yourself for a week. How often have you talked about or thought of the negatives about your job situation? When you begin to entertain a negative thought, or hear yourself saying something pessimistic to a friend or co-worker, learn to stop yourself immediately. Go cold turkey on negative thinking and talking.

3. List your expectations for the job you currently hold. Are

they realistic? A friend might help you with her objective opinion. Now rank them from most realistic to least realistic. Pick the top three and work on turning them into a reality.

Chapter 17

AS A CHRISTIAN, HOW CAN I NURTURE A HEALTHY COMPETITIVE SPIRIT?

Luci Swindoll

ne question I am frequently asked at the conclusion of a speaking engagement is, "How much did you compromise your principles when you worked for a secular company?"

My answer to this question usually surprises people since they often assume if you work in anything but a Christian company you'll be asked to behave unethically. In the thirty years I was with Mobil I didn't have to compromise my principles *once*. I was never asked to do something where I thought, I can't do this and still be a Christian. Nor did I have to personally resort to tactics that strayed from my principles to attain the position I did at Mobil. The reason in part was that from early on my co-workers knew my style—what it included and what it didn't.

Therefore, with my integrity intact, the Lord enabled me to rise from the ranks of draftsman to a department manager. I've never been intensely competitive—it's simply not my nature to claw my way to the top—but rather I worked my way up with hard work and keeping quality principles in place.

Is competition a bad word—one that can only have a negative meaning—particularly in the workplace? I don't think so.

However, a competitive spirit that is not properly used, can bring destruction rather than happiness.

———⚬———

Competition in the workplace is acceptable—as long as it brings out the best in you, which is often the case when it's personal competition. Consider athletes, for instance. Competing against one's own standards and achieved goals is what brings out winners. As a kid I was very athletic, and I remember how my own standard offered a wonderful edge against which I could strive. It kept me motivated and driven.

Keeping on Track

Once a month sit down and write out the answer to the question: What are my priorities? Then look at your actions. Are they really in alignment with what you say are your priorities? Do you need to make some adjustments? I want my epitaph to read, "Judith cared for others." I need to assess my actions monthly. Do they really say, "I care for others," or do they say, "Judith cared for herself?"

—Judith

Even today a certain measure of competition lies within me. I set goals for myself; my personal best you might say. Then, when I don't meet my own standard, I evaluate myself, rather than become jealous or envious of another who reached the goal I was seeking.

Competition, however, does have the capability of bringing out behaviors that are contrary to the Bible. Thus as you strive toward goals in your career and daily work, the main questions to ask yourself are, Can my behavior be respected? Is the way that I reached this particular goal something I can be proud of?

Remember the co-worker I mentioned in an earlier chapter who said without using intimidation to manage my staff I didn't have a chance to move ahead and be an effective manager? If I had chosen intimidation as a way to reach my personal goals, I know I could not have lived with myself.

We're headed for trouble when we compromise our faith to meet our goals. The Lord wants our obedience. And he'll get it one way or another. If you compromise your principles, you won't be able to rest at night. You'll be defensive when asked about your actions because feelings of guilt produce defensiveness. Whether you realize it at the time or not, you will be bothered by those behaviors that you know are not true to what is right or godly.

For instance, when I was a manager at Mobil I was given a company car as well as a few other privileges—a notable one was the opportunity to use my expense account for entertaining guests of Mobil or prospective clients without too much questioning. I earned the trust of Mobil to use the account wisely at my own discretion. Yet if I had lied about expenses—and this was easily an area where lying could occur and be covered up—I personally would have been very disquieted by my behavior. There is only so much you can hide inside before it rebels against you.

Mind Control

To keep competition in check, pray every day before you leave for work that you will have the mind of Christ controlling your actions and giving you wisdom.

—Mary

To say I was never without a self-serving thought in my career wouldn't be true—after all, I'm human. There were a few times I was aware that I was manipulating toward a position or hoped to be noticed for personal reasons. I'd think, I'm going to do this report and presentation to impress everyone.

But when I took stock of myself at the end of those days, I would be miserable *and* exhausted. More importantly, my sense of inner peace would vanish.

A good barometer to how competition is affecting you is to assess your sense of peace within. Am I behaving at work the same way I do with my friends, my family, my buddies? Am I turning into two different people—one personality at work and one during off-hours?

Cultivating the Servant Spirit

I don't recall a time when I had to lie, cheat, or manipulate a co-worker to move ahead in my career. On occasion, I saw others resort to those tactics as they tried to gain position or recognition. But I didn't. The reason? My goal—that which drives me—is different.

While God gave me the skills and abilities to move up to management at Mobil, I wasn't seeking the titles and promotions for a self-serving reason. As Christians, our approach to the workplace often seems foreign to a nonbeliever. We come to our job with a servant heart and attitude—our focus goes beyond ourselves to include others. We aren't driven solely by the need to meet our own needs and goals.

Competition doesn't bring out the best in us when it erodes our servant spirit and replaces it with a self-seeking attitude. And the surest way to lose your servant spirit is to let competition move from a personal level to the level where it's you against a co-worker.

There are a lot of people in life who want to be stars. They want to be in the limelight and not give credit where it's due. But as Christians, it's not our role to strive to be a star. Rather we are called to be servants. The reason Jesus could wash the feet of the disciples is because he knew he was a Prince, a King. He knew who he was before the Father. And we, too, can think in similar terms. As believers, we know who we are before Christ, and that nothing is beneath us.

I remember asking a woman at Mobil what three things in life gave her drive. The first was sex, the second money, and the third, title. Yet despite the wonderful credentials she brought to the job, within a few years her life was a shambles. Her money was gone, her marriage had ended, and her career at Mobil was over. Her desire for star status ruled her life to such a degree that she wound up with virtually nothing.

And while this may sound a little pious, I honestly believe the sooner you accept the Lord and realize that you're serving him, the sooner your diet for life changes. It comes from a completely different source.

With this diet, you want to be full, to be all you can so you have more to offer. Job tells us that he treasured God's word more than food. And in John 4:34, Jesus refers to the fact that doing God's will is his food. In each instance, the intake of Scripture provides the strength we need for daily sustenance. It's out of this strength that we make our best decisions.

For instance, if I'm living with a servant spirit within, it's amazing what happens when the promotions and perks don't come my way. Rather than fall apart or feel I've been wronged, I have a sense of peace and perspective—and co-workers notice that. I've had co-workers come up to me and ask, "Why aren't you upset by this?" and, "Why do you have such peace?"

Now, it's not that I'm never upset. But a servant spirit, which is cultivated over time, allows you to stop and ask yourself—despite the fact your heart may be aching—What did I really want it for anyway? If you examine yourself, most often the answer is for personal reasons—ones that aren't necessarily in harmony with what the Lord desires for us.

I remember once a more competitive co-worker received a promotion before I did—one I thought I deserved. While it hurt temporarily, I made a conscious effort to put the situation into perspective. In time, my chance would probably come too, and besides, my co-worker might have by all rights been better suited for the promotion.

Keeping a Servant Spirit Sound

I think it's fair to say the business world operates at a level of competition that often isn't acceptable for Christians. So how do we stay steadfast to our convictions when those around us are saying, "You won't get ahead if you don't look out for number one."

I've heard my fair share of those comments, and the best way to counteract them is to negotiate within yourself this basic issue: What do I really want and what am I willing to pay for it?

If title, position, or clout are important to you, you'll do anything for them. You'll claw. You'll lie. You'll push people down. You'll take credit for things you didn't do. But if you're true to yourself and your faith, you'll think before you act.

After you've answered the question, What is it I really

want? then ask yourself, Whom do I serve? Am I serving myself or the Lord?

I'll tell you, it can be very tempting to serve yourself if you don't have a lot of strength within. If you don't have a solid core that's based on Christ; if you don't have confidence that there is indeed something better than a title or position. And it's a tough battle to win.

How to Get Ahead

My goal at Mobil was never to be president. It really wasn't. Instead, mainly due to my personality, my goal was to have a good time and enjoy what I was doing. I've often said my favorite thing in life is to learn something new while having a good time. I wanted to laugh and have fun with my peers, to do my work in a cheerful environment. When I went about my work with this approach rather than with a competitive spirit, doors somehow opened.

I contend that if you go into a situation and say, "I'm going to be president of this company," or, "I'm going to take over my boss's job," it will drive you crazy. It will rule your life and your behavior. It will also wear you out in the process. Ultimately you end up sacrificing your character and yourself. You don't take time to be a well-rounded and balanced person. Your competitiveness makes you one-dimensional.

Besides that, you tend to live for the future. You begin to think, One day—when I get what I want—I'll make time to be well-rounded. But being a balanced person doesn't happen that way. Rather, it is a daily evolution. It is letting go of certain unattainable ideals, being honest about your strengths and weaknesses, and realizing that everyone has limitations and that not all of us will be stars.

Seasons of Competition

How competitive you tend to be about your career will be answered differently at different times in your life. My career at

Insight for Living was a second career. How I approached it was quite different from how I approached my career at Mobil. At Insight, I no longer thought, I've got to prove myself. When Insight for Living hired me, they knew what they were getting in me—good and bad.

In this situation, there was no corporate ladder. There was a sense of feeling at home, overriding a competitive drive.

As I've grown older I've discovered there are certain aspects of life I don't value the same as I did when I was younger. I used to be a goer and a doer. Now I'm starting to value tranquility and peace. I don't always have to be in the fast lane. I don't have to be out there chasing after something that I know simply doesn't exist.

The world says, "If you run fast enough and hard enough, the rewards will be yours. The titles and position will bring happiness." However, I've learned that peace and joy are truer riches.

I don't have to chase after a pot of gold. Indeed, that gold isn't at the end of the rainbow at all. Rather, it's inside each one of us, as we are transformed by our loving heavenly Father.

Make It Happen

1. Do you have feelings of resentment, uneasiness, or anger about your job? What is the source? Could it be a competing spirit that brings out the worst in you? Ask the Lord to make known to you the true source of your feelings and to direct you in ways that will remove those feelings.

2. At the end of each day, do a minireview of your actions and decisions. Were there any that left you feeling you had let God down? That you know to be contrary to what God expects from you? If that happens, backtrack and immediately question your actions. What causes you to take actions you're less than proud of? Is it a certain situation? A certain person's response? Being aware of how you respond is one of the first steps to changing those responses that aren't honorable to the Lord.

3. Look at some of the goals you have mapped out for your

career. How do you feel about them in light of Luci's comments on competition? Do any of your goals need rethinking or prioritizing to be more in line with Luci's basic questions, "What do I really want?" and, "Whom do I really serve?"

MAKING THE MOST OF THE MARKETPLACE

o better help you see your work as *both* a responsibility and an opportunity, Judith, Luci, and Mary emphasized throughout this book three principles which, in essence, are the non-negotiables for Christian women in the markeplace.

First, the confidence and strength we need to handle the many responsibilities and decisions we face each day comes from *knowing ourselves*. In the hecticness of life, too few of us take the time to consciously stop running around and take inventory of our lives. Am I doing with my life what I want to be doing? Are there gifts and abilities I have that aren't being used in my current job? These, and other questions like them, demand our time and attention. They can direct us personally and professionally. And they can help us become the person God wants us to be.

Second, in all we do, we need to *keep a servant heart*. This alone is one of the most distinguishing qualities of a Christian working woman. We aren't in the workplace to climb the corporate ladder, gain popularity, or find our identity. Instead, we're called to be Christ's love in action.

And finally, we must make certain that *God is the number one priority in our life*; not merely a distant deity we touch base with occasionally, but rather a living, loving Father with whom we can meet daily. As Mary pointed out, "Working women are busier than anyone else in the world and more tired. They need fellowship more than anyone else yet often have less time than anyone else."

Despite the temptation to put our relationship with the Lord on the back burner (along with prayer, Bible reading, and Christian fellowship), we must not give in. After all, he is our hope and strength both inside and outside the office. In him we can stand and face whatever challenges the marketplace has for us. In him, we can have peace from nine to five.

TODAY'S CHRISTIAN WOMAN is a positive, practical magazine designed for contemporary Christian women of all ages, single or married, who seek to live out biblical values in their homes, workplaces, and communities. With honesty and warmth, TODAY'S CHRISTIAN WOMAN provides depth, balance, and perspective to the issues that confront women today.

If you would like a subscription to TODAY'S CHRISTIAN WOMAN, send your name and address to TODAY'S CHRISTIAN WOMAN, P.O. Box 11618, Des Moines, IA 50340. Subscription rates: one year (6 issues) $14.95, or two years (12 issues) $23.60.